T0194852

FROM
SUDDEN DEATH
TO PARADISE

The Story of a Near-Death Experience

T.S. DISMAS

WESTBOW
PRESS®
A DIVISION OF THOMAS NELSON
& ZONDERVAN

WestBow Press books may be ordered through booksellers or by contacting:

WestBow Press
A Division of Thomas Nelson & Zondervan
1663 Liberty Drive
Bloomington, IN 47403
www.westbowpress.com
1 (866) 928-1240

ISBN: 978-1-9736-7255-5 (sc)
ISBN: 978-1-9736-7256-2 (hc)
ISBN: 978-1-9736-7254-8 (e)

Library of Congress Control Number: 2019913402

Print information available on the last page.

WestBow Press rev. date: 09/17/2019

To all the people who never gave up on my
miracle and helped me to achieve it.
Thanks for your prayers and support.

And a special thank you to my heart donor. I will
never forget you and your generosity.

CONTENTS

CHAPTER 1

It's hard to believe, but I died for ten minutes. My heart stopped for ten full minutes. Looking back on it, I am still in shock, because for most of my life I felt as if I was almost immortal. Obviously, this feeling of immortality was delusional, since I clearly did die. Death came whether I thought it could or not. I really never imagined anything capable of causing my death, except old age. I had been a military police (MP) officer in the army, serving in some of the most prestigious MP units alongside some of the toughest soldiers who ever served. I was medically retired due to injuries sustained from toxic chemical exposure. I didn't die from the exposure; I lived (for a while, anyway), but I never really gave God the credit for this. Instead, I attributed it to my personal strength. I had a couple of serious motorcycle crashes after the military, but I walked away from them virtually unharmed. I have worked with high-risk mental health patients in and out of prison as a psychotherapist, and I competed competitively in MMA and boxing. My illusion of immortality abruptly ended when I woke up in the middle of the night of August 26, 2016, experiencing the worst pain I could have ever imagined.

Before I went to sleep that night, I didn't think I was about to die anytime soon. I had a belief that no matter what happened to me, nothing would have the power to overcome my strength. I especially did not see heart failure as a possible cause of my death. So when death stealthily creeped up and ambushed me, I couldn't believe it. My feelings of immortality had developed over a lifetime, so it was reasonable to experience disbelief in those first moments of death's attack. I have survived several close calls, dangerous experiences, and brushes with death during my life, but I was about to meet an adversary of immeasurable power, stealth, and cunning. And I was totally unprepared for what lay ahead for me.

While I have been involved in many high-risk situations during my life, I was never really scared of dying. I have always felt like I have had a fighting chance or some sense of control of every situation, and because of this power I never doubted that I would survive. I expected my strength or intelligence to provide me the ability to always produce a positive outcome. I had grown certain that my death would come from something along the lines of a heroic adventure, or even simply dying in my bed of old age, but never once did I consider heart failure. Truthfully, I had hoped that something exciting and worthwhile, like saving someone's life, would be the cause of my demise. I did not expect lying on my living room couch, barefoot and in a T-shirt and shorts, to be how I met my death.

I was only forty-one years old and in great physical shape. Only two weeks before, I had a physical that showed me to be in excellent health. I was muscular and lean from a lifetime of weightlifting and running. I didn't do drugs or smoke, I rarely drank, and I ate healthy. I couldn't possibly be a candidate for heart failure. I had perfect cholesterol, good blood pressure, and a resting heart rate in the low 50s. My physical showed absolutely no signs of a heart condition. Up until this time, I ran marathons, and I had fought competitively in MMA and boxing until my thirties. I maxed every one of my physical fitness test scores while in the military, made the army boxing team, lifted weights regularly, and otherwise have been active and athletic throughout my life. So heart failure could not even be a reasonable possibility. How could it be, when I was so successful at intense and high-impact sports and exercise?

I was soon to find out that anyone is susceptible to cardiac sudden death, and one's heart function and physical health is no guarantee in preventing this vicious, silent, and merciless killer. You may have heard people say their life flashed before their eyes when they came close to death. Well, my life did flash before my eyes, except mine seemed to flash continuously over the course of the next five months. I began to see everything I had worked for slip away in slow motion, and there was nothing I could do to prevent the losses. During the next few months,

I would experience such a terrifying attack on my life that it left me completely defeated. A rare medical condition was about to commit a terrible and brutal series of attacks, determined to destroy my spirit and take my life.

CHAPTER 2

I f you struggle with believing in near-death experiences (NDEs), I can't say I blame you, because I rarely thought about them, until I had mine. I am still amazed at how my tenuous struggle leading up to my NDE permanently changed my approach to and outlook on life. I never gave a fleeting or even a curious thought to NDEs, and yet as a result of my experience, my viewpoint is now vastly different. I was clinically dead for ten minutes; my NDE was so much more profound than all my previous life experiences combined. In an instant, I became a truly transformed man. How could I not change, now that I knew what was waiting for us after this life. I want to introduce who I was before my NDE so you'll know I'm not an irrational man or a religious fanatic, then I'll tell you what I experienced and how it has changed me.

I will try to keep this introduction into my life short, because I know you're more interested in the story of my NDE, miraculously surviving my extreme medical condition leading to my NDE, and my struggle to recover, leading to my heart transplant. I want to provide you just enough background information to understand my physical, psychological, emotional and spiritual development experienced through my life up until the day of my death, January 16, 2017 without glorifying who I was or the things I accomplished. I no longer consider these early events to be as important to my life's purpose as I previously had. Instead, I view them as a few steps imperfectly taken, leading to my new life and a closer relationship with God that I gained through nearly three years of suffering, struggle, and hardship. This new relationship also demands a closer relationship with others, and I feel sharing my personal story openly is part of my responsibility to people. Although these events did contribute to me understanding my new life after I had died, they are only contributions, since I now know what is waiting for us once we die. Who I am now is based in something so much more profound than what we can experience in this life.

I was born on a fairly calm and uneventful afternoon, and maybe that's why I tried to never have another uneventful moment again. I craved excitement and adventure my whole life. My parents were very young; my mom was seventeen and my dad was eighteen, and as you can probably guess, I was not privileged with a lot of luxuries while growing up. Yet I never seemed to lack the things I needed. I certainly didn't get everything I wanted, but I don't feel like I missed out, and perhaps that made me stronger. I do remember not having cable TV or many toys like my friends, but I also learned to appreciate what I did have and to work for what I wanted. I learned to love reading, playing outside, using my imagination, and playing sports. I learned that I had to be responsible for my own happiness in life.

Not long after my birth, my little sister arrived on the scene, and I always felt she was favored by my parents. She seemed to always get more things and nicer clothes than me. I felt she had fewer chores and more freedom to hang out with her friends. I can see now that my natural happiness was such a contrast with what my sister seemed to experience that my parents were just trying to balance things out. However, once she was married and on her own, her true positive nature bloomed.

There was a significant event that occurred when we were young, and it ended up having a profound effect in shaping my personality. One day at the park, an older boy pushed my sister off the swing, and she began crying while he stole the swing from her as she lay there underneath him. I don't remember the actual event myself, but the retelling of the story by my parents had a huge impact on me while I was growing up. I was four years old, and the other boy was about 8 and twice as big as I was, but I fearlessly protected my little sister.

The story was that when I saw him push my sister off the swing, I ran to her aid and pushed this older and larger boy down. When he stood up to confront me, I yelled, "Don't ever hurt my sister again," and pushed him down once more. My parents said I told them I pushed him down the second time to make sure he got the point. The boy then ran off, but the praise I received from my parents for protecting my sister was satisfying to my young ego, and I learned I'd be rewarded with a sense of significance if I intervened to help others.

My parents praised and rewarded me, and they often spoke of my heroic actions that day to friends and family. I believe this event led to me developing a protector's mind-set, but perhaps it was already ingrained in my DNA, just waiting to be released. However it came about, I have always felt brave and courageous when defending others. This trait was validated and rewarded by my family, which ultimately reinforced this protective characteristic and supplied me with a feeling of importance and purpose throughout life.

I have always cared for other people, even strangers. Yet I had never truly understood love, probably because I never felt I really needed other people, leading to only a partial understanding. I arrogantly felt I could do everything on my own and that other people, instead, needed me to protect them but offered little that I required in return. I felt brave and courageous when protecting others, and this led to a validation of my worth, which contributed significantly to me developing a righteous protector self-identification.

When I was young, I really enjoyed learning about Jesus and other heroes of the Bible, and I was particularly drawn to David, Samson, and Moses as they fought for the rights of their people. I used to love to think about how brave Jesus was to sacrifice himself for us. During my childhood, I felt a strong connection to Jesus; my heart was full of love and loyalty for him.

Beginning around the age of nine, I began to be regularly tormented by severe night terrors. The only way I could go back to sleep after one of these nightmares was if my dad would read from the Bible, usually a story of one of my heroes. I felt so weak and vulnerable after waking from these horrific dreams that I couldn't bear being alone. I was afraid to sleep, because as soon as I would begin to drift off to sleep, I would fear being attacked by the terrors of my dreams. My dad usually chose a story about bravery and trusting in God, which always encouraged me to face those horrors I had seen in my dreams. I eventually became brave enough to return to my bed. I always slept so peacefully afterwards.

My dad was great this way because even when he had to get up early for work the next morning, he never refused to read to me until I was ready to go back to sleep. He would give me one of Mom's homemade cookies and milk, sit at the kitchen table, and read to me until I was brave enough to go back into my room. These night terrors caused me great fear of going to sleep for a couple years. I would see fearsome deaths that seemed to never end, and there was an obvious inability to control the outcome of my life in the dream. I often couldn't protect myself. It's strange, but these night terrors had the end result of strengthening my confidence in God's power to protect me; I felt a closeness with him. I learned to trust God because of those stories my dad would read.

Dad never missed work, even when I didn't return to sleep until just before he left in the morning. This taught me the value of self-sacrifice for others and the value of hard work, dedication, and loyalty. Through his example, my dad was teaching me that to sacrifice self for others was the best way to show that we care for them and an important function in serving God. He also taught me the value of hard work and dedication to your job. When I was weak and vulnerable, he would sacrifice his sleep to ensure that I would calm down, feel safe, and be able to sleep and still never missed a day of work. He was selfless to me and my family with his time, loyal and dedicated to his job. He always helped people from church and other friends. He was a great model to learn from.

I have always admired these qualities and tried to imitate them throughout my life, and they led me to great success in everything I've done. However, over those couple of years, I developed an uneasiness when going to sleep, because as I'd begin to drift off, I'd feel vulnerable to those terrors sneaking up on me. I feared being attacked by my dreams. Later in life, after growing past the night terrors, new issues developed to disrupt my sleep.

I grew up in a typical 1980s working-class neighborhood, and like most families, both my parents worked outside the home. The neighborhood kids didn't seem to have a lot of supervision while their parents were at work. It was not uncommon for the older kids to beat up on and push around the younger or weaker kids. Due to my stubborn nature and my desire to protect others, I often drew their attention, as I wouldn't give in to their demands and readily stood up for other kids. I always stuck up for my friends and often got involved when I saw other kids being bullied, whether I knew them or not. I could not seem to resist standing up whenever I saw any injustice. I learned how to fight through this real-world educational system, and the bullies were all too willing to provide me with as many lessons as I wanted to receive. I was never able to ignore the victimization of others, no matter the cost to myself. All through my life, I practiced boxing, martial arts, and wrestling, because I enjoyed the challenges they provided, but they also helped to improve the odds of my winning these confrontations, physically and mentally. During high school, this approach to injustice was strongly reinforced, and I was often involved in fights.

After high school, I left home for basic training in the US Army to become a military police officer. I wanted to continue to protect the rights and freedoms of others. I attended MP school at Fort McClellan in Alabama (once recognized as the most toxic place on earth). The base was shut down a few years after I graduated, and my old barracks looks like a decimated city after a nuclear attack. MP school is a challenging experience for all who attempt it. It is sixteen brutal weeks of training, both physical and mental. However, I thrived in this type of environment. I seemed to crave the school's discipline, structure, and pace. I won my weight class in my company's pugil pit contest and also beat the champions from the other weight classes. I then achieved the highest physical fitness score of my entire MP company by maxing out the allowable points for push-ups, sit-ups, and two-mile run, earning my physical fitness excellence badge, which is a rare feat in basic training. When I graduated, I felt stronger than I had ever felt in my life, but this led me to develop some flaws in my ego. I relied on my own physical and mental abilities to get me through challenges that life presented. This form of arrogance created less dependence on others and ultimately diminished my ability to trust other people; it also ignored the role God's help played on my life.

Shortly after arriving to my first duty station, I secured a coveted spot on the Army boxing team, and my ego really began to soar. I no longer felt like I needed God or anyone else, for that matter, and I didn't feel the need to rely on him for strength and protection. I even felt that relying on God was a weakness and believed I needed to do everything for myself. To some degree, I didn't even want him in my life, especially when I had desires that caused my conscience to become ashamed. I must clarify, though: I never did stop believing in God, and I never stopped loving him, but the mixture of my ego and my conscience caused me to try to ignore God and pretend he was not involved in my life so that I'd be free to do things my way.

During my time in the military, I experienced several events that challenged me to explain how I survived without help from God. Yet I always tried to explain away God and make myself the hero. I definitely felt God's hands on me during each one of those events, and although I tried to ignore the feeling of his involvement and attribute my survival to my own abilities, it was impossible for me to understand surviving these events without God having helped. I was never able to convince myself that I wasn't spared by God. I was part of an MP company that provided security for transport of soldiers, VIPs, equipment, weapons, munitions, and other important cargo, some of which was top secret and highly sensitive. We protected these shipments in many parts of the world, usually by train to a cargo shipping port, then often we would need to load the shipping containers onto trucks, planes, or ships and guard the shipment to a forward operating base away from the freight station. This was dangerous and important work.

On one of these missions, I was involved in an incident in which our chemical alarms went off, indicating we had come into contact with a toxic chemical agent. We immediately employed our chemical protective gear and departed the area. I was also given Pyridostigmine bromide and the anthrax vaccine prior to a deployment (I later discovered that the vaccine was not FDA approved for use on humans). After these incidents, and having been stationed at Fort McClellan, it is not a surprise that not long into my military career, I started to show signs of serious neurological and circulatory damage. I was evaluated thoroughly by the military and given a full retirement for my sacrifice. Many of the soldiers I served with had neurological, autoimmune, or other various debilitating diseases. Some of them died because of their sacrifice. During the next decade, my health seriously declined, which was related to toxic chemical exposure, a fact of life I learned to accept. I always felt proud that I overcame my injuries to some degree and was able to maintain a high level of physical fitness, despite the constant pain caused by my disability.

I learned that some injuries don't kill right away and instead take a piece at a time, slowly killing you physically and breaking your will to continue the fight. With this type of injury, it is only a matter of time before it takes you physically or mentally.

So after many years in the Army, I was honorably discharged and received a medical retirement. I was heartbroken and felt crushed at having achieved my dream, only to lose it. I didn't realize at the time that I had lived up to my desire to be a protector, and I paid a huge sacrifice with my physical and psychological well-being so others didn't have to. I couldn't see all of the people I had saved and helped; instead, I focused on everything I wouldn't be able to do. I constantly focused on no longer being able to do the only profession I had ever wanted. Being a soldier made me feel like I was significant and a valuable asset to the world.

I was still young when I was discharged, but I was in a lot of physical and emotional pain. I couldn't be a police officer, so I decided to take a year off to review my options. I focused on my recovery and to learn to live with my medical limitations. I also struggled with PTSD, but I attempted to ignore the problems it caused in my life because of my pride. Instead, I let anger consume me in an effort to protect my fragile ego. At this time of my life, I didn't understand PTSD and viewed it as a weakness; it made me feel weak and vulnerable. After having suffered so much loss and pain, I couldn't bear any more limitations.

After those years in the military, sleeping was a torment again, except with a new and more realistic twist. I now had to relive painful memories each night and then wake up to the realization that the pain I felt was real and still present. I soon began to feel the vulnerability start to take over again as I would drift off to sleep, and fear would begin to follow me like a hunter stalking its prey. Sleep had really become a serious problem now, and I got very little of it when I did at all.

I began to search for a new relationship with God, and to my surprise, he accepted me quickly and without hesitation. I felt a real sense of peace develop within me. I decided to fully give myself over to Jesus once again and soon felt a rapid lift to my emotional and mental outlook. I began to become free of my hurt, anger, pride, and self-centeredness. As these negative emotions began to dissolve, I felt at peace with myself and the world. I soon began to look for ways to help people again. As I began to change my life, the fear, anger, and shame abated, and I was renewed. I began to accept my disability but not the limitations it tried to impose upon me. These I set my will to overcome as much as possible.

I knew I would have to change everything, so I decided to take advantage of my educational benefits and attend college through the Department of Veterans Affairs' vocational rehabilitation program for disabled veterans. I worked at a factory at night while attending college during the day. I got little sleep, but at least that meant fewer nightmares. I knew I needed to find a way to be more useful in my life, and I always felt helping people was productive, so going to school all day and working all night was not much of a sacrifice. It meant I would achieve my goal and have a new purpose in life. I knew I would never be connected with my life's purpose if I didn't find some way of helping others. I quickly became hooked on psychology after taking an introductory class and decided I could help people with this new knowledge.

I was excited by psychology and drawn to providing therapy because it seemed to be a way to participate in the battles people struggled with. I felt I could assist them in their fight for peace, healing, and a better life. I knew I had been battling my medical condition and the accompanying physical disabilities, and I felt that my recovery experience would help me to be a better therapist. I also reasoned that I had always had a fighting spirit and that if I learned how people thought and why they behaved the way they did, then I could use therapeutic techniques to help them develop resiliency. I could help them to attain the fighting spirit that helped me in life and find ways of overcoming their problems.

I excelled in college and completed my bachelor's in psychology with an emphasis on addiction counseling, earning summa cum laude honors. I became a licensed alcohol and drug counselor. I was hired by the company I did my internship with and worked there for three years. My faith remained strong, and my relationship with Jesus was solid, as I could see the impact I was having on people's lives. I even worked as a youth minister for a local church. I found a mentor in Bill Wahlberg, the executive director of the treatment center. He was a strong Christian and a kind, good-hearted man with years of experience and a willingness to share his wisdom. He was inspirational; I learned a lot from him about having compassion for people who had committed some of the worst actions while in their addictions and balancing my counseling and my faith without judgment or prejudice. I learned to look not at who they were at the moment but see who they should be and treat them like that person. I found this sped up the healing process for my patients.

I realized that the sooner I obtained a master's degree in psychology, the sooner I would be able to expand my career options and help even more people. Of course, I'd also be able to better support my growing family financially. In 2009, I began a master's program in counseling psychology. As I started this program, I realized it was going to be a difficult task to work full-time, raise a family, go to school, and maintain my faith. I worked all day, went to school, and spent time with my family all evening; I studied all night, but my faith began to receive less and less of my limited time. I don't know which I did less: sleep or pray. I also stopped seeing our friends, as I had no time to spare, and while I felt many benefits would materialize from this venture, it still cost me very much. Once I reached my goals of self-improvement, I knew these sacrifices would be worth the struggle.

I completed my MA in counseling psychology in 2011 and again earned summa cum laude honors; I attributed my success to my hard work and diligence, which certainly played a large part, but I did not acknowledge that God blessed me with those traits through the experiences I had over the years. He also gave me the perseverance to see it to the end. My new degree and the experiences I had in the military helped to build resiliency, perseverance, and diligence, and I knew these traits would take me far. After earning my MA, I was immediately hired by the Department of Veterans Affairs to work with combat veterans suffering from PTSD and addiction issues. I also counseled vets on relationships, provided psychotherapy for mental health disorders, and helped vets readjust to society after serving in a battlefield. The hours were long and demanding, but I felt I was thriving as a therapist. My client caseload grew larger than my colleagues'. I soon had the largest and most successful caseload in my clinic. Before I moved on, I had the largest case load in the region.

I then obtained a position with a prison as program director for the co-occurring disorders and substance use disorder, working at a two-hundred-bed prison treatment program. I was tasked with developing, coordinating, and providing treatment for prisoners with mental health disorders and criminal thinking disorders; I also offered domestic violence counseling and addiction treatment services.

After working at the prison for two years, I started to feel worn down. I had gained the trust and respect of the inmates, my staff, and colleagues, but I wish I could have done more to secure the protection of their human rights through ethical treatment.

Working at the prison made me tired. I thought it was the long hours, so when I was recruited for a clinical supervisor position in a growing private treatment program working with the same clientele, only outside of the prison walls and bureaucracy, I took it. This program had a mission statement of putting clients first and treating clients and employees fairly and respectfully; the job also came with a significant increase in pay. When the position was officially offered, I decided it would allow me more opportunities to do good and that it would be more consistent with my personality and my high standards of honor and integrity.

I began my new position on May 1, 2016, and was making a lot of progress, helping the team in advancing our program's mission and goals for growth. I was working fifty to sixty hours per week for the 126 days leading up to the most impactful event of my entire life. The next four months would prove to be the most challenging of my entire life. I was about to learn more than I had ever cared to learn about cardiac sudden death, cardiac sarcoidosis, and eventually heart transplant. I never thought this could happen to me. Nothing else had ever come close to the severity of the physical and mental pain I would experience. I experienced pain, mental anguish, fear, loneliness, sadness, and vulnerability, and my toughness, determination, optimism, and perseverance would be challenged like never before, until I turned my will over to God and accepted these things as they were.

I had lived my life with the belief that in order to be worthy of God's love, I needed to be constantly pleasing him through sacrifice and always working to become more religious. I was to learn that I cannot make frenzied efforts and hope to accomplish true peace. Accomplishing a goal is only momentary; the feeling of satisfaction cannot last for very long, and soon another goal will be needed to regain the feeling of significance. I was to learn that loving God and truly caring about others is the most important purpose in life. I have faced so much adversity in my life, and

I've never failed to stand up and fight back against any injustice, but I missed many opportunities to use that strength to help people change their corrupt actions.

Instead, I viewed the commandments as advisories and didn't allow God to show his love through my interactions. I wanted to be viewed as heroic, a protector of the vulnerable and defenseless, but I never worked to help the bullies. I might have stopped the aggressors for a moment but never changed them. I did not see how bearing suffering, and always staying in a mind-set of love, is the only way to live in harmony with nature and God's will. I was about to receive a profound lesson.

CHAPTER 3

On Friday, August 26, 2016, I woke up at my usual time, around 5:30 a.m., and got ready for my workday. For the most part, I felt fine; I was a little tired, but working long hours as a clinical supervisor of a large treatment center, serving criminal offenders, is enough to wear anyone down. I finished my high-paced, grueling day a little after five and started for home through rush hour traffic, still feeling tired, but I was excited for my daddy-only weekend to begin. My wife Tina had already prepared dinner for the kids, said her goodbyes, and left for her family's cabin for a girls' weekend shortly after I arrived home. She was excited to see her family and to do a little wild mushroom hunting in the deep woods of northern Minnesota. My daughter Ann (thirteen), my oldest son Elijah (eleven), and Joseph my youngest boy (eight) were all set to begin our fun weekend by having an end-of-summer campout with some slightly relaxed rules, playing usually Mom-banned games like moonlight hide-and-seek and Nerf gun wars.

Suddenly, out of nowhere, in the darkness and silence of the night, everything changed. I woke up around midnight, feeling sick. Actually, it's more appropriate to say I was viciously sick; my chest was pounding, and I had trouble breathing. I quickly noticed that my heart was beating harder than ever before, even while competing in sports or exercising. In fact, it was beating so hard that I started to throw up violently. This was no doubt the worst I had ever felt in my entire life. It felt as if someone was stomping upon my chest. At first, I thought it might be food poisoning, and then it even crossed my mind that it might be some new kind of super pig/cow/mosquito flu, but it never occurred to me that it was heart failure. Elijah was so concerned that he slept on my floor the rest of the night, holding a puke bucket each time I threw up; he cleaned that bucket each time I filled it. Ann got me a cold wet washcloth and wiped the sweat away from my face.

By the next morning, I was no longer throwing up, but I was barely able to breathe; it now felt as if a very heavy person was stomping up and down with both feet directly on my chest. The pain was so intense that the room was spinning, and I felt like I was going to pass out.

I was a strong, muscular man and in excellent physical condition. I was used to my kids wrestling with me, using all their strength and never holding back, as children often think their dad is indestructible. They would even jump from the couch and land with knees first, directly onto my chest or stomach, but I have never experienced pain like what I was feeling now. To put my pain tolerance into perspective, I was once kicked in the chest during an MMA bout and cracked two ribs in the opening seconds of the first round. I didn't go down and was able to continue to fight, and I won the three-round bout with broken ribs. Despite the pain and difficulty breathing, quitting never crossed my mind. However, I was now feeling more pain and had more difficulty breathing than I had during that fight. The pain I was feeling was relentless, and I could do nothing to stop it. I had no means to fight back and no hope of winning.

I thought I might feel better if I got up and went out of my room to get some fresh air. I decided to go downstairs and lay on the couch. However, as I attempted to walk, I was unable to catch my breath, and the pain made it too difficult to walk. In fact, I actually couldn't walk. I couldn't breathe, and I could barely see. I was dizzy and light-headed, and I was seeing spots; the world seemed to be spinning around me, causing severe tunnel vision.

I decided to slide down the stairs on my butt. I then crawled the rest of the way to the couch with the aid of my kids. It felt like I was crawling across a bumper car arena, and I was the main target of the other drivers, except I didn't have the protection of a car. My children began crying, and I realized that the situation was worse than I originally considered. I had to admit that I might die very soon.

I didn't feel better being downstairs; instead, my condition seemed to get worse. I texted Tina and told her I was going to die. She suffered from panic attacks for years and insisted I was most likely having a panic attack, trying her best to reassure me that I was not going to die. She later said she was upset with herself for not having the kids call 911 immediately, but that's how hindsight gets us all. I also wished I had called sooner, perhaps in the middle of the night when it all began, because doing so may have spared my heart additional trauma. I just never imagined I was experiencing heart failure while it was occurring.

I am a psychotherapist with expertise in treatment of PTSD, trauma, and addictions; I work regularly with clients suffering from panic attacks. I was certain this was not a panic attack due to the intense physical pain I was suffering; I believed I was going to die very soon. I just couldn't figure out why I felt so bad. I was uncertain of what to do. I had never called 911 before, and I hesitated calling for fear and embarrassment, if it was not as serious as I thought. I thought about a saying from my training and experiences in the military: There are two kinds of people: the quick and the dead. The quick act; they are decisive and often live because of their decisive action. On the other hand, the dead hesitate to act and often don't react; their fate takes them without so much as a struggle. I didn't want to be the dead, but I was conflicted and didn't want to overreact, either.

While I worked as a military police officer in the Army, I had seen many serious injuries, so I knew how serious my condition was. My breathing was so labored and difficult, and the pounding in my chest became so painful that my vision was becoming blurred. The room seemed to be spinning at an incredible rate, and I was close to passing out. I now knew my situation was critical and if I was going to survive, I needed immediate medical assistance. I didn't want my kids to see me die like this, so I gave Elijah my phone and told him it was okay to call 911 now.

He was unable to make the call because he was crying so hard, so he gave the phone to his sister, and she bravely made the call. When the police officer arrived, he took one look at me and called for a rush on the ambulance; my condition was critical. The living room was soon full of first responders and paramedics with hurried and seriously concerned looks upon their faces. I knew my situation was really bad, but I still didn't realize the problem was my heart. I knew my chest hurt, but I thought my heart was reacting to some other condition.

I didn't think for a second that my symptoms were from heart failure; I stubbornly endured the pain for several hours until finally allowing my kids to call 911. My attempt to tough it out and not ask for help exacerbated my condition and severely reduced my chances of survival; it could have caused additional injury to my heart. Perhaps I endured the pain because the strongest of my core beliefs was to never be seen as weak. I thought if I called for help and then my problem turned out to be indigestion would make me look stupid and helpless. At that time, that was the worst possible situation I could imagine.

CHAPTER 4

After the paramedics arrived, they took my vitals and then immediately prepared the automated external defibrillator (AED) so they could start cardioversion. A cardioversion is a high-powered jolt of energy, an electric shock, to my heart in order to slow my rapid pulse. When I saw them place the paddles on my chest, I knew my heart was failing; they told me I was in serious ventricular tachycardia (VT). They said that my heart rate was running about three hundred beats per minute (BPM), and they needed to stop this fast arrhythmia by shocking me out of it. They explained that this was necessary to stabilize my heart prior to taking me to the ambulance and transporting me to the hospital. They said they were convinced I was about to go into cardiac arrest at any moment.

I was stunned to hear that it was my heart causing the problem; I couldn't believe this was heart failure. I remember saying, "No way; really? It's that bad?"

The paramedic responded "Yes, it's that bad. Your heart is beating too fast and not pumping enough blood to your organs and extremities. Your body is shutting down."

They told me that if they didn't get my heart under control, I would certainly die; they needed to get me to the hospital as quickly as possible. They explained they could not risk moving me until they had lowered my heart rate. I felt like I was going to die at any moment, and suddenly fear overtook me. I felt I was absolutely powerless to change anything. I knew I was completely at the mercy of my fate. I felt I needed people for the first time, and this caused me to feel totally vulnerable.

I looked at my children through the sea of emergency personnel, huddled in the hall; all three were looking as if they knew I was going to die. They looked stunned and were crying; it was heartbreaking to see them like that. It was as if every ounce of hope had been ripped out of them, and their spirits were crushed and broken.

I now had tunnel vision, and everything else faded away. Their faces suddenly became clearer, and they were all I could focus on. I was thinking this might be the last time I see them, and it looked as if they were having the same thought. The looks of terror on their faces was agonizing, and it is permanently burned into my memory.

I barely had time to tell my kids that I loved them and that they were the best kids a dad could ask for. I couldn't bear to think of how life would be for them without me. The looks on their faces ran repeatedly through my mind. My kids then were escorted outside by some of the first responders.

As they were heading out the door, Elijah yelled, "I love you, Dad; you're the best Dad ever." Ann told me that she loved me and would pray for me, and little Joey just looked blankly into space; tears streamed down his tiny face as he gasped for breath between sobs. The love of my kids brought me a strange mixture of comfort and agony, so I resolved to refocus my attention on fighting for my life.

Just then, I received a violent shock from the AED, bouncing me like a fish freshly pulled from the water. After the shock, I remember saying, "Good morning. That hurts," but I was feeling somewhat better, and my heart rate went down enough to transport me to the hospital. As I began to breathe a little more easily, I asked the paramedics to give me "another jump," as I was hoping to keep the VTs from returning. They told me the one had worked well enough that they could start the IV, give me medication, and transport me to the hospital; they could provide more emergency services in the ambulance, if needed. The paramedics asked which hospital I wanted to go to. The VA hospital was quickly dismissed because I didn't feel comfortable going there for heart failure; I asked the paramedics which hospital they recommended and chose one they suggested. I felt only a miracle could get me through this situation. The pain was so intense that I faded in and out; I don't remember anything after this point, even though I was conscious until the doctors sedated me hours later.

CHAPTER 5

After I texted Tina that I felt like I was going to die, she began the three-hour drive home from the cabin. Ann called to tell her that she called 911 and relayed all the conversations with the paramedics. Our friend who lived nearby took the kids to her house. Tina was still in shock and denial that I was dying. She knew I was so healthy and strong, but when she received a call from my doctor about the severity of my situation, then it all became real. He told her that they were trying to get my arrhythmia under control. He explained that she should hurry if she wanted to see me because most patients in my condition didn't survive; it didn't look as if I would make it much longer. She was so worried the entire drive back to the Twin Cities, wondering if I would still be alive when she finally got to see me. She called my parents, and they immediately started to drive up from Georgia. Other family members and friends began prayer groups with their churches and friends. I would later learn that while I had felt alone, I actually had more support than I could have ever realized. I think this had a huge impact on my survival. It also showed me how wonderful support from other people really is.

The next couple of hours were more stressful, painful, and terrifying than anything I had ever previously experienced; thankfully, I have no memory of those terrible hours and only know what I was told by medical personnel afterwards, but I felt so terrible that I knew it was as bad as they explained. My heart still couldn't pump the blood necessary for my organs to function properly. Soon my liver, kidneys, brain, and other organs were beginning to suffer heavily from the lack of blood, and they began shutting down.

I was later told that I resolved to fight off death and refused to give up. I told the doctors that I felt a sudden surge of courage and strength that came from some reserve of additional power beyond myself. I can't imagine having the strength to make it through on my own. I kept saying I was a fighter and always have been, that I have never backed down from a challenge and that I would win this one too, but deep down, I felt beaten. Everyone kept telling me how strong I was, and I desperately wanted that to be the truth, but I knew I was not this strong. The situation seemed hopeless, and I felt I would not find a way through this.

I cannot explain where the courage and strength I found came from, as I don't even remember what happened, but I really do believe that God gave me the strength from all the prayers I was receiving. Later, I must admit that I credited my tenacity and physical strength for successfully surviving my heart failure. I minimized the protection provided by God and the prayers I received, but I knew I had been beaten and was very fortunate to survive. I guess I just wasn't ready to give up my false sense of control.

During all of this, my heart's ejection fraction (its ability to pump blood) dropped to less than 10 percent, and my liver, kidneys, and other organs began to fail. My breathing continued to decline; the doctors decided to anesthetize me and insert in a breathing tube, as I was quickly approaching respiratory arrest. I had to be strapped down when they attempted to insert the breathing tube; I was fighting against having the tube inserted in my mouth. As they tried to put it down my throat, I broke the straps loose and had to be held down; they were worried I would keep breaking the straps loose as they attempted to insert the breathing tube.

Finally, just prior to my going into respiratory failure, I was successfully medicated and intubated. I cannot recall anything while they continued to diligently work to save my life through the night, but I now know that I had fought a very serious heart failure incident for about fifteen hours. God was obviously working on my behalf, because my condition was even more serious than anyone knew. I survived my first heart failure incident; the cardiac sudden death was caused by an underlying condition of cardiac sarcoidosis. Few people make it through this condition.

CHAPTER 6

Later that evening, after my heart rate slowed, the doctors told Tina that my ejection fraction was still below 10 percent; my liver and kidneys were still failing, and my vitals were barely detectable. I would not likely survive the night. They felt that if I did survive, it would not be for long, and the best-case scenario was I would never leave the hospital. They told her that she should consider the end-of-life decisions for when the time comes. They feared that I was going to be brain-dead in a few hours, so even if I did survive through the night, I would likely be in a vegetative state. It seemed impossible for me not to have serious brain damage caused by the lack of oxygen to my organs, particularly my brain. They were monitoring my brain activity and seeing very discouraging results. This would not be the only time I would defy medical odds. The doctors said I'd never have a normal life again; in a way, this would prove to be true.

Tina later told me she knew I was a fighter, and she was determined to give me every chance to fight as long as I was clinging to life. She was extremely worried because the doctors had warned her that she'd have to make end-of-life decisions in the hours to come; she didn't know what to do. She stayed with me as long as they let her that first night and encouraged me to keep fighting. She later said she may have threatened me a little as well, because she couldn't imagine telling the kids that their father had died. That would be a terrible message to share, and I'm grateful she was spared that conversation. I don't have any memory of her words, but her encouragement, along with the prayers I was receiving, somehow resonated with me and encouraged me to continue to fight.

The doctors told her that she might as well leave because there was nothing more she could do, and they needed to run more tests during the night to fully determine the damage and recover some of my organ function; she decided to head for home. She knew she would now be facing the most difficult discussion parents can have with their children.

When I woke up, I felt like I had never been alone and that someone had been by my side the whole time. I was confused but not scared, and the fear was gone. I began having moments of consciousness starting late Sunday afternoon, but I didn't fully wake up until late Sunday evening. I felt as if I had just been hit by a truck, and then the truck backed over me so the driver could take a look at the damage he caused, and finally, the driver decided the damage was too serious to help and turned it into a hit-and-run by spinning out the tires on me before running me over again during the getaway. I felt terrible, and at that time, I preferred not to be awake.

I was covered with IVs, breathing tubes, and heart and brain monitors. I had no idea where I was, until a nurse explained that I was in the ICU and had barely survived a very serious heart failure. I have never felt so physically weak, intellectually feeble, and helpless in my entire life. In fact, for the first time in my adult life, I was truly uncertain of what was happening, and I had no idea what I could do. I prayed seriously for God to help me through this, but I felt like such a hypocrite, praying for help now, when for so long, I thought I could live my life without God's help. I wasn't sure God would be interested in listening to my desperate death bed pleas, but I still hoped he'd be forgiving, because he always forgave people in the Bible. I could hardly move on my own, and I knew my situation was still very serious and beyond my control.

When I first woke up, I wanted nothing more than to have the breathing tube removed immediately, because it was so uncomfortable, and I couldn't talk. Honestly, it was causing me so much anxiety being hooked up to all the machines, and the breathing tube was the worst because it prevented proper communication and made me feel totally helpless. I felt the breathing tube had to go so I could ask some questions. I wanted to know what had actually happened to me.

I motioned for something to write with and was handed a pen and paper. I was very weak from the intense battle for life and the extreme pain, and I had little body control, so my scribblings were difficult to read. I was unable to spell correctly, my thoughts were hard to explain, and I couldn't write legibly. I was able to get the doctors to explain the reason for the breathing tube and how long it would take to have it removed. My vote, obviously, was to immediately remove it, as I was close to removing it on my own if they did not. When they did finally remove the breathing tube, they also removed a large thick IV from my groin. They explained the condition my heart was in and told me about the head and other monitors that were attached to me. I was hooked up to so many devices, IVs, and monitors that I quickly became anxious again; when the doctors explained how serious my condition was, I thought I was going die. I felt as if I might die at any moment.

I asked the doctors to give it to me straight, and not candycoat anything, because I felt I needed to know what I was up against and what my odds for survival were. So they explained that I suffered so much trauma to my heart and other organs that they were in danger of failing again, at any moment. I was also told that my heart, liver, kidneys, and brain would likely have permanent damage; if I was to survive, life for me would never be as it previously had been. They said as I could see by my inability to write I had suffered severe brain damage, maybe even a stroke. The doctors told me I was lucky to be alive due to the extreme seriousness of my situation. I was also told I should accept the fact that I was going to be in the ICU for a very long time and in the hospital for months. They said I still most likely would not survive.

I asked Tina how the kids were doing, and she said they were scared and extremely traumatized by what they saw. She told me they were relieved that I was alive and wanted to come see me as soon as they were allowed, but she thought it would be too much for them right now. I wrote the best I could for Tina to call my office, let them know my situation, and tell them I would be back as soon as possible. This was important to me because I felt keeping my eyes on returning to my normal activities would help me to recover more quickly. I knew that my mind was stronger and more intact than the doctors thought; I just couldn't communicate that to them yet. I had lost a whole weekend of my life. I felt like I had just gone to bed Friday night and that it was only a few hours ago. It was strange to me that it was now late Sunday night, and I would not be going to work the next day as usual. I would now miss my first day of work in years. I never missed work because as the clinical supervisor, I felt a responsibility to ensure my staff was properly prepared to provide therapy services to our clients.

I was confused and growing scared, but I tried to not show my fear because I had no control over the outcome. I also did not want to show any sign of weakness, which might scare my family further; I could see the terror on their faces already, and I grew more concerned that my situation was still life-threatening.

My parents arrived, and my mom began talking about miracles and needing to stay positive, but it was over the top at that moment and really frustrated me. Her behavior and comments were even noted in my medical records, as I would later discover, because it was disrupting the doctors and other medical personnel, who were trying to explain things to me. While I was in that condition, her miracle talk was more annoying and discouraging than helpful and motivational, as she genuinely intended it to be. She didn't realize that the talk of miracles was distracting, because I didn't feel worthy of a miracle, and so it brought my mood down. The only thing I wanted to focus on was trying to fight through this situation.

It wasn't like I didn't feel God could assist me, but I strongly believed he required more of an effort on my part. For so long, I relied on my own powers (or so I thought), and I believed he might let me suffer a little to remind me of my human frailty, but in reality, he had already miraculously saved me. This would happen many times over the next couple of years.

I soon became frustrated with my mom. She struggled to understand my written messages, and she continually interrupted the doctors to express how God would miraculously cure me; this was a big distraction. I could see the doctors were also getting frustrated with her behavior, as they were trying to save my life and had medical decisions to make, with no time to discuss miraculous possibilities that in their opinion were not likely to occur.

I know she was scared about my condition, and her comments were as much to help her deal with the severity of the situation as it was as an attempt to keep me positively motivated, but they were distracting and quickly became intolerable. So I wrote, "Get me a translator," in hopes that she would stop talking so I could fully understand what had happened to me, what I could expect to happen next, and what was required of me to recover. I realize she was extremely worried and probably tired from driving from Georgia to Minnesota, but she was making it impossible for me to understand my situation, as I couldn't stop focusing on her. I needed medical answers right now, so I could figure out what I needed to do; I needed to communicate my concerns and get questions across without these distractions and interruptions.

CHAPTER 7

I slept off and on most of the evening after first waking up, only occasionally waking up when the doctors and nurses came in. When Tina and Ann came to see me I was asleep, but very happy to see them when I woke up. Tina slept on the couch in my room and didn't have a chance to get much sleep that first night. She was ready to comfort and encourage me each time I woke up in pain, all through that night. On Monday morning, when the doctors came in to check my progress and found my brain function to be vastly improved, they admitted that they were surprised and had no medical explanation. Since in the span of one night I had already recovered beyond their expectations, they found it difficult to explain my medical problems in depth and wanted to run more tests. They still weren't ready to call it a miracle, but they did say it was a medical miracle.

None of the diagnoses made much sense to me. I was trained in psychology but lacked the medical training to understand my condition or its severity. The more the doctors described each condition, I realized that they were right; I was lucky to have lived. I also realized that my mom was correct: Each breath I was taking was a blessing from God. I think my survival was actually the miracle my mom was hoping for, but it was still too early for her to see that. I knew my survival was not due to my ability to fight though this; I certainly did not will myself to live, even though I was struggling to admit that I had nothing to do with my survival. Basically, I should not have survived that first heart failure, but somehow, I did, and believe it or not, my real fight was just about to begin.

Over the next couple of days, I was told several times by many doctors and specialists that I should expect to be in the hospital for months. Those first couple of nights provided me some time to think about this grim outlook, and I decided to learn what I needed to do to be cleared for discharge. I was going to fight so I could do it as quickly as possible. I desperately wanted to go home. The doctors told me that if my ejection fraction and liver/kidney functions improved to a sustainable level, they'd be willing to discuss other benchmarks for discharge. They stressed that I should focus on surviving right now, because I was not out of the woods just yet and was setting myself up for disappointment.

I think some of the doctors initially took a look at my tattoos and determined that I was a drug abuser; they gave me little of their time and seemed to be indifferent to my care. They had the pharmacist check with my pharmacy upon arrival, considering my age, healthy physical appearance, and the symptoms I was experiencing. I certainly think that is a wise and prudent approach. The hospital pharmacist found my medications and blood levels were well within my prescription parameters and revealed that I only took my medications as needed and had no illegal drugs in my system; the team of doctors ruled out chemicals as a cause. This news seemed to help some of the doctors change their opinions of me; their dispositions did improve, but honestly, I picked that hospital because of their experience working with difficult cardiac situations often caused by chemical abuse. They truly save lives that most other institutions would be unable to save.

My doctors also explained that they were surprised that I had not suffered serious brain damage due to the lack of oxygen and blood flow caused by the duration of my fight for life. They were uncertain about how much permanent damage I would have and how it would affect me; they said it would take time to determine the extent of the damage to my brain. They were even more surprised that the brain scans and monitors showed no major loss of function, considering the length of time my brain endured decreased blood flow and low oxygen levels.

They then told me that with the damage done to my heart, I'd need to have a defibrillator implanted in my chest to shock me out of future VTs (I also had to take medications to prevent the VTs from occurring). They said they needed to wait until my heart stabilized before it could be implanted, but it was important to have it done as soon as possible.

I asked if my heart would heal, and they said it may improve some, but there was significant scar tissue showing on my MRI and CT scans; the severity of the damage would determine how much healing could be expected.

As the days progressed, the doctors remained baffled by the unbelievable progress I was making in recovery. They were still surprised that I had survived at all, let alone improved as much as I had. They were shocked by the progress I had made in such a short time. In fact, they were even more surprised, given my preliminary tests. In reality, it was amazing for anyone to survive the serious event I just had. My mom and dad were still talking of miracles of full recovery, and looking back, I have to admit that it sure seemed more plausible that there was a miracle at work. I received no medical rationale for my survival and started to believe it was God's desire to keep me alive.

The doctors said that my situation appeared to be viral myocarditis, but no virus was detected, so they assumed my body had already cleared it out, leaving only the scar tissue behind which had caused the VT arrhythmias. The many tests administered showed significant damage to my heart, with massive scar tissue everywhere; they couldn't tell me how long I might survive, if I did at all. They could not guarantee that I'd survive the next few days. They were still certain I would be in for a long stay at the hospital and many months of rehabilitation after that, if I ever left at all.

I resigned myself to survive and told myself I would fight my way through this. I knew I couldn't control whether I lived or not, but I could control how I looked at it. I refused to rely on the doctors to get me through this event. I started to thank God for getting me through my extreme heart failure and asked for courage and strength to endure the recovery process. I began to pray more and feel more positive, but I had to resolve the sense of distance I had created between God and myself. I think I felt this way because of the arrogant way I had lived my life.

My parents, especially my mom, continued to interrupt and talk about miracles every time a doctor came into the room. The staff seemed more annoyed at each visit, as they needed to explain my status and the next steps in the recovery process. Still, she insisted that I would have a full and total recovery and my recovery would happen because of this miracle she expected from God. I was becoming more irritated at this point, because these statements interrupted my conversations with my electrophysiologist, cardiologist, and other specialists. I wasn't so annoyed when she did it to some of the other medical care team members, as they had treated me with indifference anyway, so I was happy to see them leave more quickly.

I think many of the doctors felt underappreciated because she believed God would cure me; they were also struggling to discover what actually happened to me. This of course was true; they had no answers, and their best treatments were not seen as effective from the beginning, but this was not their fault. I was fighting a very complex condition, as would be discovered later. She seemed to dismiss their medical efforts, as if they were not needed, and her interruptions still caused me to be distracted. I felt that I often failed to gather information fully, but mostly I felt it diverted me from putting my intentions into improving as much as possible. I wanted to get better so I could be medically cleared to go home. In order to go home, I needed to know exactly what was going on with my body medically and what the doctors needed to see in order to clear me.

I missed my kids more and more as the days pressed on. Due to my weakened condition, they were only able to visit for brief periods of time. I really was too weak to comfort and encourage them when they were able to come, anyway. Ann and Elijah were hesitant and timid when trying to hug me. However, Joey was still innocent enough to think his dad is some kind of superman; when he saw me alive, he was comfortable enough to jump into my bed with me. I was relieved that he didn't appear too traumatized by the situation. I was a little discouraged by the fact that I still appeared as weak as I felt, even though I thought I was doing a good job masking it for their sake. I wanted to reassure them (and maybe myself) that I was improving more than I was feeling. I wanted to remove from my mind the image of their faces as they stood in our hallway the last time I saw them. I thought I was presenting as pretty stable and healthy, considering all I had been through. My intention was to look like I could fight my way through this. I think I was only fooling myself and my youngest. Everyone else knew the situation was very grim.

I was encouraged when the tests of my heart function showed no structural or mechanical concerns. My veins, valves, and arteries were functioning well and were clear of even a drop of plaque; there was no need of any type of heart surgery at this point. My heart was healthy except for the electrical system damage caused by the event and the remaining scar tissue. The doctors still believed this situation to be caused by the mysterious viral myocarditis. This was explained to me in the following way: At some point, I had a common virus that we are all exposed to, and this virus attacked my heart, which caused weakness in my heart's cellular structure, which led to the VTs. This in turn caused the scar tissue and damage now present in my heart. The scar tissue that remained was most likely worsened due to the length of time I battled the heart failure before seeking medical assistance. Arrogantly, I had begun to pride myself on the point that at least I did not show weakness and call for an ambulance too quickly, but that only proved to be a fault I learned to overcome. Trying to be so strong and tough sure didn't pay off, and now I'd have to settle the bill. The payment was to be infirmity and humility!

Over the next couple of days, many amazing and unexplainable improvements occurred. Perhaps my mom knew something I didn't about the whole miracle thing. My kidneys and liver improved drastically, my heart began to stabilize, and I was able to leave the ICU. By September 1, doctors said I was stable enough to have the defibrillator implanted. The next day, Friday, September 2, a defibrillator was implanted on the left side of my body. By surgery time, my liver and kidneys had completely recovered, my brain had no significant damage, and my ejection fraction had improved to 20 percent.

The doctors were perplexed by the speed and level of my recovery. They admitted again that they couldn't explain it. I think they were additionally confounded because of their inability to explain what had happened to me. I felt guilty for feeling so irritated by my mother, but I didn't want to admit the possibility that she may have been right, so I remained indifferent in accepting this as a miracle. My mother always told me I was capable of doing anything I wanted, as long as I worked for it. This built up my self-esteem but also contributed to my self-reliance and my difficulty accepting outside help. On the outside, I said I beat death because of my strength and determination, but on the inside, my weakness and fear tormented me, as I knew I was only alive because of the grace of God.

The implantation surgery went well, and there were no complications. I had improved so much that I was released the following evening, September 3, with my ejection fraction now just under 30 percent.

CHAPTER 8

When I was finally cleared to go home, I was still in extreme pain from the heart failure itself, multiple cardioversions, and other lifesaving techniques used during my heart failure event, and the surgeries and tests during my stay in the hospital. Now the additional pain from the implant surgery added another level of discomfort and slowed my movements even further, but I wanted to be at home while I healed. I felt my recovery would be improved around my family, and I also believed that my kids would recover from their trauma more quickly if they could see me every day. So I toughed it out and minimized my pain levels (of course, if I am being totally honest, I wanted to present myself as one tough dude, anyway). I thought breaking all the medical records and doctors' predictions and getting out of the hospital so soon after having had such a serious heart failure would make my family feel more comforted and help us to return to our normal life. I also needed to believe I was tough enough to survive this ordeal.

When I first got home, my kids were really helpful, and Tina drove everywhere to get me medications, special food because of my new low-sodium diet, and other comfort items. I was too uncomfortable to sleep in my own bed, so I slept in the guest bedroom; Elijah refused to let me sleep alone because he feared something might happen if no one was there to check on me. He told me he needed to be with me in case I needed assistance, and then he promised he'd be able to call 911 this time. It was easy to see that he was immensely traumatized and needed to feel safe for himself, as much as keeping me safe. I truthfully didn't want to say no; having him there actually made me feel safer. He took such good care of me and waited on me hand and foot: fluffing my pillows and getting me water, food, or reading materials. I mean, he did the whole works and gave me the full treatment, which made my recovery much more tolerable, almost enjoyable, because I felt so loved. My little Joey had been unable to sleep alone since my heart failure and had been sleeping with his mom; he still refused to sleep alone after all that he saw. All the children were traumatized by the experience, and I was at a loss about how I could help them through it.

The first week was extremely difficult. Mostly, I slept. Then as my mobility returned and my strength improved, I began taking short walks around the neighborhood. I extended my distance a little more every day. My intent was to return to full health and to be cleared to drive in a month so I could return to work again. My doctors told me to expect to have driving restrictions for up to a year; the restrictions could be lifted within a month, if I demonstrated I could be medically safe on the roads.

I have military retirement health insurance (Tricare), and my doctor prescribed cardiac rehab to improve my heart function. Even though it was deemed necessary and requested by my entire cardiac team, I was told Tricare would not provide this coverage. Since cardiac rehab was required and could be provided at the VA hospital, I called the hospital; the staff said they couldn't provide cardiac rehab due to my age and the type of heart failure I had. Believe it or not, they said it may someday correct itself, and they had too many patients waiting to receive care. This was more of the VA being mismanaged and unable to properly serve veterans. I knew I was on my own, which was nothing new, as most veterans have experienced a lack of care and coverage through the VA.

I worked hard to rehabilitate my heart and did physical conditioning on my own, but it was scary to raise my heart rate without the proper measurement tools and medical personnel to ensure my safety. I had several appointments over the next few weeks, and at each one, I blew my doctors away with the progress I was making. I was eventually cleared to drive and returned to work on October 3, only a month after being released from the hospital. I was so excited to return to normalcy. I was feeling stronger again and walking a couple of miles per day, lifting some weights, and doing push-ups; I only required a couple of short naps during the day.

During one of my walks, I took a short break and enjoyed nature, which I was now seeing in a different light. I looked down and noticed something I'd never found before, perhaps because I was taking things a little more slowly and enjoying the moment. At the time, I had been thinking about how blessed I was to be alive, and right then, I found a four-leaf clover. I had heard that a three-leaf clover was like the Holy Trinity: God the Father, Jesus, and the Holy Spirit. So I started thinking that a four-leaf clover must be a symbol of the Holy Trinity and me. It represented my connection with God. I certainly felt this was true at that moment, and I started to believe that God had forgiven me.

I later learned that traditionally, the first leaf of a four-leaf clover represents faith in God; the second is for hope in salvation through the sacrifice of Jesus Christ; the third is for the love shared and available to us; and the fourth is for luck (or perhaps a miracle), which could only describe my situation. I was lucky to be alive, I was lucky to have God's mercy and love, and I was lucky to have forgiveness and salvation waiting for me whenever I finally died. I now think that the fourth leaf represented me, because luck can only relate to the experience of the person experiencing it.

I was so excited, and my courage really soared because as a little kid, I always searched for four-leaf clovers but never found one. I stopped looking as a teenager and never cared as an adult. Now spontaneously finding one when I wasn't even searching, but really needed inspiration, was incredible. I feel God was trying to tell me something.

CHAPTER 9

Elijah still refused to let me sleep alone, and since I was still uncomfortable in my bed (and truthfully, my snoring would keep Tina awake and then she would wake me up), it was more comfortable in the guest bedroom. My colleagues were getting impatient to have me back, as we were going through a merger, and my experience on the clinical leadership team would make or break the deal. Twenty-four days after I got out of the hospital, my CEO sent me a text telling me he needed me to get back to work; he offered me a percentage of the company once the sale went through. I felt a lot of pressure to return to work. So a month after getting out of the hospital, I begged my doctors to clear me to return to work, even though it really was too soon. As soon as I returned, I strengthened the structure of the program for the sake of the merger, which had been put on hold due to my absence. I worked hard those first few days (maybe a little too hard).

Three days after returning to work, early in the morning of October 6, I was abruptly awakened. It was 4:45 a.m., and it felt as if someone had just hit me in the chest with a baseball bat. I saw a flash of light, as my body forcibly crumpled in half, and my knees hit my face with such force that they caused severe bruising. I jumped up, unable to breathe, and my chest was throbbing. Elijah ran down the hall, screaming for Mom, because he knew something was wrong. I was certain, beyond any doubt, that someone had just hit me with a bat; I thought our home was being invaded. So I struggled from room to room, looking for the perpetrator.

My heart was beating so fast from what I thought was the adrenaline, and my chest and face were throbbing in extreme pain. I was so anxious about what had happened that the longer I couldn't find the cause of the blow, the more my fear for my family's safety grew. I managed to check all the doors and windows. Every one of them proved to be locked and secure, with no sign of forced entry. Tina, Ann, and Elijah were screaming for me to come back upstairs and lie down.

Tina thought I had been shocked by the defibrillator and wanted to send in a remote test report. So she called the device clinic line to tell them what happened. The power and force of that shock was so painful, from my waist up to my head, that I couldn't believe it. I wondered if a defibrillator could send such a devastating surge of electricity throughout my body without killing my still weakened heart. It was so intense that I can only compare it to being hit by a baseball bat, swung by a power hitter. It was more powerful than a stun gun and way more painful. Of course, I was lying perfectly still and peacefully asleep in my bed, not expecting to receive such a discourteous awakening. It was terrible. I could see by my family's reactions that even though I felt like I was improving in my recovery, they were no longer convinced. My weakness must have seemed very apparent to them at that moment, and they looked as if they were terrified that I would still die. I now began to question my strength and health. How could this have happened? I felt like I had become so much stronger lately.

Stubbornly, I went to work at my normal time that morning. I felt compelled to go into work, because I had just got back that week and didn't want them to think I was weak or that I was only trying to collect my short-term disability insurance or secure my percentage of ownership in the company. Later that morning, I received a phone call from the device clinic, telling me I had to come in immediately. I was told that they were worried that my device had inappropriately delivered a shock, and they needed to determine what had happened. They had to test my device to see what adjustments needed to be made to prevent more inappropriate shocks. They also needed to check my vitals to ensure I was medically safe, since I received such a powerful shock. I finished conducting morning therapy groups and left for the hospital during lunch.

During the interrogation process, while two nurses and a representative from the device manufacturer were going over the data, I received another inappropriate shock; this shock was so powerful that my knees buckled again and smashed into my already bruised and swollen face. I almost fell off the examination table from the force of that shock and went into a life-threatening ventricular tachycardia heart rhythm. About thirty seconds later, my device fired again, and I once more received a powerful explosion in my chest, except this shock brought me out of the life-threatening arrhythmia.

While I was in the military, I felt powerful explosions from close proximity, so what I say next is not an exaggeration. These shocks felt like a bomb just went off inside my chest. Once my heart was stabilized, the ER charge nurse began arguing with my doctor and the device manufacturer rep, stating that I needed to go to the ER for observation per hospital policy and given my condition. The doctor and device rep did not want me to go to ER, but the charge nurse won the argument, and I was taken to the ER for further evaluation and continued stabilization. The manufacturer rep came along to monitor my device and gather information about what had gone wrong. I was scared; my device had misfired twice, and those shocks caused me to go into a life-threatening arrhythmia. It could happen again. I questioned whether these shocks caused more damage to my heart, especially since they caused me to go into VT. If it happened again, I didn't think I could endure it. I thought I might die from the very device the doctors were counting on to keep me alive. It was like holding a live grenade and wondering if it would go off (I've also experienced holding a live grenade, but at least I was able to throw it).

A code 9, code blue, or whatever is the hospital's emergency code to indicate a life-threatening situation was occurring, was called. After the code 9 was called, the entire examination room was filled with doctors, nurses, and other emergency personnel; even the hospital police came to assist. I was given oxygen because I was having a difficult time breathing from the shocks (I'm sure that the small room being full of people didn't help).

I was brought to the emergency room to be stabilized for the rest of the evening, even though my doctor and the device manufacturer rep still protested. The ER doctors and charge nurse insisted that I must be evaluated and monitored, since my heart still was not stabilized. They insisted that the ER was the most appropriate place to stabilize my heart, and I agreed, effectively ending the argument. The ER doctors warned me that I had just suffered three serious shocks, called an "electrical storm"; the trauma this caused my heart would take a toll on my heart and body for the next few days. They said I would likely have pain and discomfort in my heart and chest, as my heart attempted to recover from the force of those terrible shocks. An electrical storm is a very serious issue and causes severe cardiac trauma. I was basically electrocuted, just barely a month after getting out of the hospital, after having survived a serious heart failure. This seemed to make the electrical storm even more concerning.

After a few hours, I was able to convince the ER doctors that I was healthy enough to go home and did not need to stay in the hospital overnight. I promised that I would return if I began to feel any symptoms. My health seemed to decline quickly from this point. The doctors were absolutely correct, as I was in extreme pain for several days afterwards. I now felt terrible again, and I was so weak that my positivity and strength drained from me.

Of course, I couldn't sleep for fear of receiving another shock, so I decided to research the internet for possible answers as to why I was shocked. During this inquiry, I verified that three shocks delivered in a twenty-four-hour span of time is indeed considered to be an electrical storm, which is a very serious medical issue. I became more concerned about my doctor having argued with the ER charge nurse about keeping me in the ER to be monitored. It sure did feel like I had been caught in an electrical storm, and I can only imagine that being hit by powerful jolt of lightning, right in the heart, is the next worse thing to these shocks.

I was later told that since my defibrillator was a new technology, this was the first instance of an inappropriate shock being delivered. They had many theories about what had caused my shocks but no definitive answers and would need to monitor my case closely. They said the first of the inappropriate shocks may have been caused by movement, but during the device interrogation, the device had recognized the movement and registered nothing unusual about it. According to my doctor, it should not have delivered a shock. There was not yet an explanation for the second shock I received in the office. The initial suspicion was the interrogation equipment picked up radio frequencies that were interpreted as VTs requiring therapy. The shock during the interrogation was recorded as a perfect five-digit code being received by the device. The way it was explained to me is that normal therapy delivery occurs once a run of 100,000 digits over thirty seconds, demonstrating sustained arrhythmias, requiring a lifesaving shock to be delivered. That shock appeared to be caused by a malfunctioning interrogator, which told the device to bypass the safety mechanism and deliver the violent shock. I received this shock, which caused my heart to go into VT, and the device read that therapy was necessary and fired to shock me out of the VTs. These shocks were delivered at the device's full power. I was so afraid that it might kill me.

Months later, I learned that the programmer for the interrogation process on my device had been recalled by the FDA. This recall occurred on February 9, 2017. I was not told about the recall by my doctor or the device manufacturer; instead, I heard about it while receiving care at Mayo Clinic. The programmer did, in fact, pick up radio frequencies and then triggered an inappropriate shock. I was the first person in the world to receive this type of inappropriate shock, and the manufacturer said they used my data in their attempts to reengineer the technology and to improve the therapy for others (so perhaps at least some good was to come from this unfortunate event). The first three shocks were like explosions directly in my chest. It was so painful that I was petrified of having the device in my body, ready to explode yet again, at any moment. From that first electrical storm, I felt an instant decline in my health.

I was unable to exercise after the electrical storm and found myself physically and mentally weaker. I got exhausted more often and more quickly than before the shocks. It was as if I was literally fried from those shocks, and perhaps I was. I was again terrified to sleep because each time I started to drift off, I feared being shocked again. This inability to sleep was reminiscent of when I was a kid with night terrors and then again after my experiences in the military, suffering PTSD-related dreams. Due to my service-connected disability and the accompanying experiences, I was terrified of what appeared to be a new dimension of disability, and I felt it was going to take my life. I was unable to sleep at all for three days after the electrical storm.

On the fourth day, I took a sleeping pill and finally found some rest, but not for very long. Over the next couple of weeks, I experienced severe

PTSD and high anxiety from those shocks. The PTSD from the electrical storm was more severe than the PTSD I had related to my military experiences. My heart and overall conditioning were deteriorating rapidly. I had to check my heart rate every few minutes and worried I'd be shocked again at any moment.

My test results showed I was at a high risk for further sustained VTs, so another Holter monitor was ordered to see if the aggressive medication changes were suppressing the extreme number of premature ventricular contractions (PVCs) I was experiencing. The monitor results showed that I had over forty thousand PVCs, with five hundred runs of nonsustained VTs; while this test showed that my heart function continued to deteriorate, the final analysis ultimately resulted in my situation being a high risk for continued VTs and future heart failure. I cannot dismiss the fact the electrical storm was a significant contributor to my decline in health, but a more serious condition was at work and had gone undiagnosed. I felt weak and scared, and I began to pray furiously. The worse my health got, the harder I found it to sleep, because when I would start to drift off to sleep, I would feel vulnerable, and panic would set in. I could not sleep until the sleeping pills finally knocked me out, and at times, they didn't work at all. Of course, the lack of sleep and the stress from anxiety about my health didn't help my heart to recover any faster; in fact, they seemed to have the opposite effect, but they did encourage me to pray more, and my relationship with God seemed to improve.

CHAPTER 10

Due to the rapid decline of my health, my doctor recommended that I travel to a hospital in Cleveland for heart ablation surgery. He told me that he would initiate the referral process with a doctor he had trained under and whom he felt was one of the best in the world at what he said was a unique procedure. He also said that if the ablation surgery was unsuccessful, I would need to consider a heart transplant due to the instability of my heart rhythms. He told me I had a high risk of heart failure and sudden death, and I may die if I didn't get a transplant. I was at first reluctant to have the ablation surgery because as it was explained to me, the doctor sends a catheter up through the groin into the heart and burns the space around the part of the heart containing the scar tissue that is triggering the arrhythmias. This is done to remove the space between the scar tissue and healthy tissue, which eliminates the bouncing effects triggering the arrhythmias. The PVCs were coming from multiple areas of my heart that also happened to be very sensitive and risky. So there was no guarantee that they could get them all. It was unlikely that the surgery would be effective in eliminating the vast amount of PVCs, but it should provide me some relief. I agreed to this procedure because I was terrified of a heart transplant and wanted to avoid that at all costs.

The electrophysiologist told me that he had completed his residency under this great surgeon at the hospital in Cleveland and knew him on a personal level. He told me that if a member of his family needed to have a similar type of surgery, he would send them to this doctor, whom he would recommend for the surgery, especially with the complexity of my condition. He added that since they already had a relationship, there would be better follow-up and consultation after the procedure. My case and medical history were reviewed, and the date for the ablation in Cleveland was set for December 7 and 8. I was concerned I might not make it long enough to see the surgery, as I was feeling weaker every day. I set my mind to not only making it to the surgery but recovering successfully, and I prayed daily that God would see me through the surgery.

So Tina and I purchased tickets and booked the hotel from December 6 through December 11, as the hospital advised I would not be cleared to leave until a day or two after the surgery to ensure proper healing. My health had been deteriorating so quickly since the electrical storm that I felt I would not live much longer. The trip would prove to be expensive, and the time away from my kids and work were going to be difficult, but I hoped to finally find relief.

The pre-op appointments showed significant PVCs and nonsustained runs of VTs; when I met with the doctor, he explained why my situation was such a high risk. He then told me that ablation was too risky for me due to the various locations of the PVCs; ablating those areas could cause further damage to my heart or lead to additional medical complications, including a stroke or death. He seemed reluctant to proceed with the operation due to the extreme complexity of my condition and did not seem confident he could perform the ablation successfully. I felt my optimism begin to fade with every word that fell from his lips, and while I did expect him to tell me about all the risks associated with ablation surgery, he appeared to lack the confidence to handle my case. After he initially reviewed my case, he told me I was a perfect candidate for surgery. He explained all the complications at that time and still felt the best option was to proceed. Now after this change of direction, I began to wonder why my doctor was so taken with him. I also began to question his integrity.

I would have preferred for him to tell me the procedure was too risky prior to my flying to Cleveland from Minnesota. After all, he had my medical records detailing the very same concerns he now listed as possibly too risky; these same records had already been reviewed by him and his team and discussed with my doctors prior to them agreeing to take on my case. He now presented as hesitant and unsure. I grew alarmed and anxious at his lack of confidence and unwillingness to proceed, even though he had assured me I needed the procedure prior to my flying to Cleveland.

I was instructed to take my medications as normal the night before surgery and to still take my heart rhythm meds the morning of surgery. I thought this seemed irregular, because if he was to determine the exact areas triggering the PVCs and VTs, then why have me take my medications, possibly preventing effective readings? So I asked him if the medications would prevent proper analysis, and he said he wanted me to continue my meds to prevent arrhythmias if we were unable to complete the procedure. I'm no doctor, but I thought this explanation described how these medications would blunt his attempts to elicit the arrhythmia triggering areas that he would need to ablate. In hindsight, I wonder if this was a calculated attempt by the doctor to limit my PVCs and VTs so I would not have any arrhythmias. Given his reluctant disposition the previous day, I feel he didn't want to admit me into the hospital for observation, either, so he had me take my meds.

I entered the clinic at 6:30 a.m. on the morning of December 8, signed authorizations and filled out paperwork, and sat to wait for the twelve-hour operation to begin. They then brought me into a pre-op prep room that resembled a stable in a horse racing park, with several stalls containing other patients preparing to have various surgeries. The nurses then prepped me with electrodes on my chest connected to monitors, IVs, the whole works, and soon they were checking my PVCs, which demonstrated a short run of VT as soon as the monitors were hooked up, with many PVCs to follow, about every ten seconds, and several short runs of VT, all through the prep time.

Around 7:30, the team of doctors came in to explain how the surgery would proceed, and then at eight o'clock, they transported me to the operating room. The doctor said he was uncomfortable with the various locations and frequency of my PVCs and VT runs, so he decided to administer adrenaline in an attempt to isolate the origination points of the abnormal rhythms, instead of putting me under and inserting the catheter to manually stimulate VT, as was originally planned. I was still awake at this time and told the nurse I had been expecting to be put to sleep prior to the procedure, and the doctor would map the trigger points to ablate once inside by manually stimulating them. She said she didn't know why the doctor was proceeding the way he was, but that he must have a reason. The first dose of adrenaline did not help isolate any specific areas. Then a second dose was given, but oddly enough, the doctor said this was not effective, either, and according to him, it seemed to slow the arrhythmias.

After merely one hour of monitoring my arrhythmias, the doctor came to tell me that he was uncomfortable proceeding with the surgery because he felt the risks were too high. He said he felt more complications could be caused than problems solved. All of this without putting me to sleep and inserting the catheters into my groin and up to my heart, as is the normal procedure. This felt like a death sentence, as I already felt like I was dying leading up to this surgery, and I now had to walk away without any relief and no prospective treatment.

The assisting doctors could barely hold eye contact with me while the lead doctor stammered through his explanation; he had great difficulty answering my questions and referred me back to my primary doctor for further answers. The assisting doctors and nurses appeared disappointed; they were being denied the opportunity to help me, and this decision was obviously not fully agreed to. When I pressed for more answers, the doctor quickly excused himself and told me he must go because he was needed elsewhere. I asked how that could be possible since my surgery was planned for eight to twelve hours. He said that I should look to quality of life, not quantity, and left without explaining why he needed to leave.

After the aborted ablation surgery, Tina and I were at a loss of what to do next. I became dejected and started to believe I was going to die, if even this highly recommended heart specialist couldn't help me. Up until the electrical storm in October, I had felt I was strong enough to get through this. I told Tina that the way I was feeling now, I didn't think I would make it another month.

She then told me that when the doctor called to tell her to come back and pick me up, he told her, "You should focus on quality, not quantity, of life."

I thought about that statement, "quality not quantity," all night. How could a doctor say such a thing without even trying to live up to his Hippocratic oath and the promise he made to help me, not even attempting to provide any relief? I was mad that he said this to Tina, as if she didn't have enough to worry about. I was already feeling like I was not going to make it long without a medical intervention or a miracle. Perhaps both were needed at this point, but to say that I should focus on quality not quantity and then to not even try to ablate some of the trigger points left me feeling that neither quality nor quantity were possible at this point.

I felt hopeless and was concerned that I wouldn't have enough time to help my kids understand the severity of my condition and prepare for my death. I was also upset about being stuck in Cleveland, with no way of getting home to have some of the recommended quality with my kids, and it was also severely limiting my quantity with them as well. My blood felt stale and lifeless, barely coursing through my veins, and my body felt as if it was going to shut down at any moment.

That night, I told Tina that I felt my blood was stagnant and not circulating and said I felt I would die very soon. I broke down completely and could not see how I'd survive long enough to ensure my family would be prepared before my death. I might not make it to Christmas. I was angry that I wasted a lot of money and time in Cleveland for absolutely no results, simply because the doctor wouldn't even attempt to treat me as previously discussed. My fears had become a very real prison in which I was mentally confined. Without the strength of my body and due to its physical decline, my mental strength left me too. I was so sure that each tomorrow would bring doom and devastation. I lost sight of the blessings of today and mentally stopped living.

A severe snowstorm hit Cleveland the day of my scheduled ablation and was still raging when we boarded the flight home. I was so physically and mentally exhausted from the trip that I kept dozing off in the airport.

The next day, Tina had scheduled an appointment to get a second opinion from a cardiologist at a hospital near home. I was so tired by the time of the appointment, I wasn't sure I could make it, but I was desperate to find a doctor willing to help me, so I went anyway. This doctor felt there was nothing he could do to help, because my condition was not his specialty; he referred me to yet another doctor, a colleague of his who was more knowledgeable about my condition. He told me that he was unwilling to do the ablation and could not guarantee his colleague would be willing to work with me, either.

My primary cardiac doctors now seemed to abandon me; they did not call me to discuss the Cleveland results, and as far as I knew, they had no follow-up plans. I called to schedule the follow-up appointment myself, and they could not see me until after the New Year began. Additionally, no other doctors were willing to work with my arrhythmias. I was convinced that I was not going to make it until the New Year without some kind of intervention. I felt as if I was dying and getting closer to death every moment that passed. In fact, I felt very strongly that I would not live until January, maybe not even until Christmas. I felt so alone and realized only God was able to help me through this, but I wasn't sure what he wanted me to do.

CHAPTER 11

E arly in the morning of December 14, just a mere five days after the aborted ablation, I received another terrifying and painful shock. That morning, at 3:45 a.m., my device fired again, and I received another powerful shock, as if a bomb just landed on my chest without any warning. The shock was so powerful that it bent me in half and shook me out of bed, depositing me swiftly onto the floor. The defibrillator produced a powerful shock. Elijah was with me again; he screamed for his mother and hugged me as I lay crumpled in pain and fear. The fear that sets in after a shock isn't simply because of the pain of the shock itself, but also of the fear of getting another; it was also terrifying to think that your heart may be failing.

Ann and Tina came in to help calm me down. I could not sleep the rest of the night; Elijah stayed up watching movies and talking with me. We sent in a remote monitor report to my doctor, but I only received a message back from his nurse, confirming that I did receive a shock (no kidding; I knew that), but unless I received another shock, I didn't need to come into the office. I still felt terrible and thought I was going to die, I just received a shock and since there was no apparent concern about this shock, I was not given any further information. My doctor never called me back to discuss what this shock meant to my health or to follow up after the aborted ablation. I questioned his investment in handling my case. I had messaged him that I was feeling close to death, but he never responded to me.

I felt weak, tired, and scared, and I was certain that this was a sign of more problems to come very soon. I could literally feel my body dying, but no one was listening, or they were unwilling to help me. My doctor had recommended I go to Cleveland, despite how close The Mayo Clinic is to my home. He should have taken my concerns more seriously. He told me prior to setting up the surgery that he felt ablation surgery was needed immediately. However, having the ablation aborted and with no follow-up plan or response to this recent shock so soon after traveling to Cleveland, I felt my doctors were basically leaving me to die. I knew I needed help but felt I had exhausted all options. I was still feeling as if my heart was getting worse, and I realized I was on my own. I felt I may only have a few days until my heart would give out again, and this time for good. I began to pray diligently to Jesus and asked for his strength and protection to help get me through this terrible situation.

I contacted Mayo Clinic that morning and sent my medical records to them. They assembled a care team and responded the next day; they arranged three days of tests and an ablation surgery two weeks from the day they called. They had scheduled the ablation surgery just in case they felt I needed it after the tests, so we wouldn't need to wait. I suddenly felt I had some hope again and believed that if only I could survive for the next two weeks, I'd be helped by these doctors, who were willing to try to relieve the issues with my heart, which would give me a better chance to fight whatever was happening to me. Mayo Clinic is clearly the number one hospital in heart and overall health care in the world, and I wished I had gone there immediately. They have a stellar reputation and superb success statistics, but they are also willing to take on high-risk and challenging cases like mine, while the hospital in Cleveland was not. Mayo Clinic didn't make me wait an unreasonably long time for my appointments when I was facing a life-threatening medical condition. This dedication to the patient's medical needs demonstrates they care about people needing medical assistance.

The stress these arrhythmias placed on my heart was like running several marathons each day, and I certainly felt like I had been. The added difficulty of such a task was that my heart was operating with less than half of the functioning capabilities of a normal heart. My heart was barely supplying my body with enough oxygenated blood to sustain life, but not enough to add running marathons on top of it all. I felt doomed if something didn't change very soon. Tina and I were both becoming concerned that my doctors were purposely avoiding me; they were unsure of what to do next and had also come to the conclusion that I would not live much longer. I thanked God for helping me to get into Mayo Clinic so quickly and for giving me hope again.

Then it happened again, five days after the shock upon returning from Cleveland and just ten total days after the aborted ablation. I still did not receive any communication from my doctor, and now I was in for another painful and life-threatening heart failure event. The days leading up to this event were some of the most painful, exhausting, and miserable of my life. I was to face fear, death, and pain unlike I have ever felt before, and I would question my chances of survival and see my desire to live come into question.

CHAPTER 12

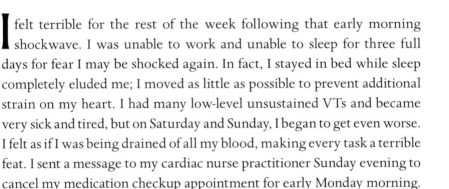

I felt terrible for the rest of the week following that early morning shockwave. I was unable to work and unable to sleep for three full days for fear I may be shocked again. In fact, I stayed in bed while sleep completely eluded me; I moved as little as possible to prevent additional strain on my heart. I had many low-level unsustained VTs and became very sick and tired, but on Saturday and Sunday, I began to get even worse. I felt as if I was being drained of all my blood, making every task a terrible feat. I sent a message to my cardiac nurse practitioner Sunday evening to cancel my medication checkup appointment for early Monday morning. Judging by how I felt, I didn't think I would be up to an early morning appointment and then having to drive through rush hour traffic across the Twin Cities to get to work. At this time, I really felt like I needed to be at work, because I felt the patience and support from my company dwindling rapidly, and my family's savings were taking a substantial hit.

I arrived to work around 6:30 a.m. and was at work for about an hour and a half when the first shock nearly knocked me out of my chair. It was so sudden that it seemed to come out of nowhere. The force of that jolt made my knees hit my desk, but at least hitting the desk saved me from more bruising to my face. I received no warning that this shock was going to come. I had felt sick and tired, a little short of breath and dizzy, but otherwise okay prior to this electrical bomb blast. I called the heart clinic right after I recovered from the shock, but I had to leave a message and wait for a return call. Again, I was told I did not need to come in unless I was shocked again or my symptoms worsened. I did not feel any better, and I was now super dizzy, light-headed, and short of breath, and my heart was hurting. I guess this did not count as worse, but I sure thought it should.

My boss asked me to leave and told me I needed a new medical clearance before returning to work. This was despite my doctors telling me that I did not need to be seen. I could sense my employer was viewing me as a liability, and they were concerned that I wouldn't survive this problem. They wanted to replace me to protect themselves in case of injury in the workplace. They insisted that I leave and go to the doctor immediately, but they refused to call 911, because of confidentiality concerns for our clients. They did not want to draw negative attention to the treatment center with an ambulance showing up. Since my doctors were not concerned this was an emergency, I figured I would just go to the ER. I really was in no condition to argue and just left and went to my car.

I barely made it to my car. I debated calling 911 myself, but the treatment center where I'm clinical supervisor is located in the most dangerous part of town, and all our clientele were felons; my employer did not want the negative publicity, and I decided to follow their request and not cause more issues with my employment. The HR reps were very cold in their request and insisted that it would be best for the company, so soon after the recent merger, to not have negative publicity. I left and began the perilous drive home; once home, I planned to have Tina drive me to the hospital.

However, five minutes into the drive home, I received another shock. I was barely able to keep the car straight and remain in my lane. I was luckily traveling against rush hour traffic, but the highway was still pretty busy. I was driving on the interstate, and let me tell you, I quickly discovered the saying about people being "Minnesota nice" is just that, a saying, but not always true. I say that, because as I tried to pull over to the shoulder, I received many middle fingers and yelling of words with obviously unpleasant intentions. The worst part was one man was actually preventing me from accessing the exits by speeding up and slowing down, blocking my way intentionally, so I missed the exit to a nearby hospital. Then three more shocks followed, spaced about ten minutes apart. I started to believe this was the end; I was going to die alone on the interstate, either from my heart stopping or from being fried like a moth in a bug zapper. I knew I couldn't take much more and remain conscious. Each shock was draining my energy, and I was near collapse. I began praying for God to get me through this.

As I received those additional four shocks over a twenty-minute span of time, I began to worry about losing consciousness and being in a crash on top of the electrical violence and extreme pain I was enduring. I couldn't imagine what was wrong with my heart to cause so many shocks. I know the other drivers had no idea what I was going through, and while giving me the middle finger and muttering obscenities about my driving isn't nice, I can understand their frustration, as I was definitely erratic. With this many shocks in such a short span of time, I knew that my condition was very serious. I needed to exit immediately and call an ambulance. I knew I would be unable to make it home, and then I had a fourth shock, which almost knocked me out. I was finally able to pull into a parking lot of a church, where I could easily explain my location for the ambulance.

I had been talking with Tina on my car's speaker system as I was driving; when I hung up with her, she immediately jumped in her truck and drove to the church I was parked. I then called 911. The police arrived almost immediately, but they were afraid to touch me because I looked like I was about to die at any moment; they asked me to remain seated in my car. They were probably afraid to get shocked, and I really can't blame them; they didn't want me to move and trigger another shock. The ambulance arrived within minutes, and the paramedics started IVs to stabilize my arrhythmias and transported me to the hospital within minutes. My vitals were extremely concerning, and they were amazed that I was still conscious; truthfully, so was I. Tina arrived shortly after the paramedics and talked with one of them long enough to give a detailed account of my condition and medications, while the other paramedic gave me some medications to stabilize my heart, along with morphine to ease the pain and Ativan to control my anxiety.

The ride to the hospital seemed to take forever, and I anxiously prepared myself for another violent detonation of my defibrillator. After that first shock, my heart had begun to feel seriously injured and sore. Since the second shock, I could now recognize the VTs as they arose prior to shocking me the next four times. I was having regular runs of VTs;

the medication was preventing them from lasting long enough to lead to another shock, at least for now. I was light-headed and dizzy; I was short of breath, and my heart was racing. The inside of the ambulance was now spinning so fast that I started to feel sick.

The paramedics told me that most of my arrhythmias seemed to be short runs just below the 220 BPM threshold of my device to initiate therapy, but then suddenly, they began to ramp up, and then another ferocious shock was delivered. During the ambulance ride, I was still thinking I wasn't going to make it through this situation, as my body seemed highly charged with electricity, and my heart was pounding. I was having respiratory difficulties, and my blood felt motionless, like my heart was not pumping a single drop. In fact, it pretty much wasn't. Every part of my body was screaming in agonizing pain because of the lack of blood flow. I didn't think I could endure another excruciating shock. I prayed intensely that another shock wouldn't sneak its way in. I felt as if my blood had stopped circulating altogether, and as fast my heart was beating, it was actually pumping less blood. I recalled that this was what the approach of death felt like. I felt like I would definitely die if I had another arrhythmia requiring another shock.

Upon arriving at the ER, I was rushed into a critical care room. They continued giving me heavy-duty medication infusions. Suddenly, I felt my heart getting worse again, and the medical staff began to rush around and call for more personnel. Then I received another blast from my defibrillator, right there on the ER table. It bounced me upright, and I almost fell off the table. This additional shock, the sixth of the day, nearly knocked me unconscious again, and I began to drift off. I was barely able to fight off unconsciousness for several minutes; my head was spinning after enduring the electrical quakes. My heart was beating fast but not pumping blood, and I was in a desperate condition. For several minutes, I felt as if I'd lose consciousness at any moment.

I believed I would not live through another shock. The doctors told me the situation was dangerous, and they had to call the cardiology specialists to discuss critical care. The ER doctors were able to contact my cardiologist and my electrophysiologist to discuss my history and ask for suggestions. They were too busy to come down the hall and assist personally with my case; instead, they told the ER doctors to stabilize my arrhythmias with medication and sedate me if they couldn't stabilize me.

The device manufacturer device rep, however, did arrive; she came into the room, eager to interrogate my device. Her presence during this emergency situation felt quite inappropriate to me, as I was hooked up to devices monitoring my heart already. I was busy fighting for my life and felt that her desire to check my device could have waited until later, especially when she reported that my doctors had called her to apprise her of my situation; they had time to call her but didn't take a minute to come and stabilize my heart in person.

She showed me my device printouts and said I received six shocks.

I said, "No kidding. I felt them."

She then tried to explain why I was receiving the shocks due to the high arrhythmias.

"I know," I said. "That's how a defibrillator works."

I already knew that my device operated under these parameters, but she was not able to give me any medical explanation as to why I was having the arrhythmias (she was not part of my medical team or hospital personnel responsible for my care).

She did, however, say she was surprised I didn't lose consciousness, and she was even more surprised that I was able to drive while receiving the shocks. She said it was remarkable that I was able to retain the sense of mind to pull over where I did and contact the ambulance, given the combination of my heart rate and the shocks I was receiving. Pulling over and calling 911 certainly had saved my life. She confided that the situation with my device was the most severe that device manufacturer was working with on that device. She told me that the data from my case was leading to move the technology forward. She said they were trying some fix some bugs in the technology and perfect the therapeutic value of the device, and my case would be instrumental in preventing others from suffering inappropriate shocks. They were now referring to my case to improve quality care, which made me happy that something positive was coming from my suffering. I was not receiving explanations or follow-up from my doctors on how this was affecting me and my device, and that was very frustrating.

I stayed in the emergency room for a few hours so the doctors could be sure my heart had stabilized enough to transport me up to the ICU. I was now on the most powerful heart medications via infusions; I still did not believe my body could physically tolerate another shock, and I was convinced my heart would not be able to withstand one, either. I was growing tired from the frequent runs of VTs I was having, despite the medications, and I was worried about another shock. I was sick of hearing doctors and nurses trying to reassure me by saying, "Well, at least the defibrillator worked to save your life." I never found this comment to be helpful, because while it saved my life, the flip side is, my condition was bad enough that it needed the defibrillator to save me in the first place. I realized the uncertainty in their eyes gave away the fact that they too believed another shock may kill me, and they had no idea why I was having all these VTs. So the defibrillator was a double-edged sword and presented a painful and frightening situation nonetheless.

The ER doctors consulted with my cardiologist and electrophysiologist about what course of action to take. The ER doctor told me I was fortunate to still be alive, but I was not yet out of harm's way and still might regress. She told me that they were doing everything they possibly could to preserve my life and return my heart to its normal rhythm, but my arrhythmias were from various locations, and they were so complex that the medical staff was unable to pinpoint the triggers.

Neither of my heart care team doctors came to the ER to see me or assist with my care. I knew it was up to God to save me. I became angry and disappointed at their apparent lack of concern for me as a patient; perhaps they feared they could not adequately provide me proper care. However; these feelings led to a reinforcement of my need to rely on God to survive, so I am actually thankful. I really started to feel closer to God and began to think that maybe this continued medical ineffectiveness was turning out to be a gift.

I realized that I had been surviving this with minimal involvement from my doctors already. Except for prescribing me medications, they didn't seem to have any idea on how to treat my complex condition, anyway. They had no idea what was causing my condition, for that matter, and had not discovered the correct diagnosis. I knew that if I was going to live through this, I was going to have to get through it without them.

I did still wonder if it was God's will for me to survive or not, but no matter what he had planned for me, I needed to accept it and be at peace with it. Worrying only caused fear, and the fear led to increased heart rate, which in turn might cause more arrhythmias, and that could kill me. I sure didn't have a clue about what I could do to change things, so I tried to convince myself that worrying was not going to help the situation. Not worrying is easier said than done, until you truly put your life into God's hands.

CHAPTER 13

L ater that afternoon, once my heart became fairly stabilized, I was moved to the ICU. I was told that I needed to remain in the ICU for a while and that once my heart stopped producing sustained arrhythmias I would be moved to the cardiac critical care unit. I was told I would be staying in the hospital until after Christmas and then transferred to Mayo when I was stable enough to be transported. A heart transplant was again mentioned as perhaps the best intervention to reach a positive prognosis for my survival, but I still got no explanation for the underlying cause. I was told my chances of living for a year had significantly decreased even more now that I had the double electrical storm on top of my already extremely damaged heart, and their inability to discover what was causing my condition only compounded my fears. The doctors were still uncertain of and perplexed by the mysterious root cause of my heart problems. They still insisted that my heart problems were related to the significant scar tissue they detected in previous testing, but they couldn't explain why I now had more scarring. Lacking another cause, they were confounded on how to proceed to treat me appropriately. At least they finally admitted that they were uncertain and felt Mayo Clinic was my best option.

I was losing patience and had no confidence in my medical team. I prayed hard throughout my hospital stay that more evidence leading to an accurate diagnosis would surface. I could see I needed to rely on God's strength and his plan for my future more than ever because my doctors couldn't help and my strength was almost bankrupt. I had to do this, or I was going to worry myself to death. I was receiving prayers from everyone I knew (and even from many people I didn't know yet). I was so thankful for all of the prayers because I could actually feel the effects of their care, concern, and kindness. These prayers from others proved to be a major reason I survived. I continued to have moments when I felt unworthy of God's intervention, thinking I hadn't done enough to show him that I loved him, but he was obviously helping to sustain me, and I felt it.

I was anxious that more shocks would come every time I had VTs, which was still very often. I was especially hypervigilant when it got quiet at night and I was alone. I couldn't sleep at all. Over the last few months, I had been through so much, and each time the situation and my chances of survival grew decidedly more desperate. I kept trying to keep my focus on fighting through it, but I still struggled against my old belief in my own strength. I knew I had to make an effort to survive, but I was now learning that God was willing to help me make up the difference. I just had to do my part.

I had to admit that I had no control over the outcome. I had to focus on what I could control, and if I did, I believed I would succeed in the end, no matter the outcome. As a result of my doctors' lack of answers, I was tested by depression, anxiety, and anger. These emotions clouded my judgment and negatively impacted my disposition. I was regularly asking myself why this was happening to me. How could it be happening, considering I had been so healthy and in great shape? I had always thought I was a good person, I worked with people no one else wanted to work with and I always helped people throughout my life, so why was this terrible situation happening to me? I had to let go of it all and just accept my situation.

I had a lot of time to think in the hospital room, and I realized fear wanted to conquer my faith and distract my focus on recovery. It kept sneaking doubt about my strength and about my worthiness of God's mercy into my thoughts, preventing me from focusing on the fight for my life. Fear was at times successful in its attempts to disrupt my prayers, and this seemed to be a precursor to more VTs. But fear could not stop my prayers completely, and I continued on, like a skilled mediator, despite fear's constant assaults. I could always feel God's presence when I focused on him or asked for help, and he encouraged me to hold onto my courage and fighting spirit, and in doing so, they strengthened my faith.

Much of the time, I felt physically weak, mentally exhausted, anxious, and totally helpless. These emotions kept me wavering in my communication with God, as it was hard to pray while fear rolled endlessly through my thoughts. I also found myself trying to call upon my pride to fight against these emotions as I had in the past, and I tried to tell myself that I was too strong to die like this. The problem was, I didn't really believe I was strong anymore. I needed to find a new source of strength. The more I realized my faith was my strength, fear was all too willing to try and lead me closer to anger as a distraction, and then the anger would lead me back to my fear.

I was angry at my cardiac team when they did not come to see me, for their lack of answers, and for their failure in treating me. I was angry about the uncertainty of my life and my situation. I was just angry. This anger disrupted real conversation with God as much as the fear, because now my prayers were becoming more like demands than requests. I always felt I had a fighting chance in life, even during the close calls and other brushes with death I had, but not now. I knew I needed to accept the uncertainty and embrace whatever was in store, as it all was part of life and my path. I felt that God might be allowing me to feel helpless and weak so I could learn to trust in him and feel his unconditional love instead of my personal strength. God's love resounded in my soul so loudly and powerfully after I finally relinquished my need to control the situation and turned it over to him. I began to feel some peace, and it encouraged and strengthened me. I found myself readier than ever for whatever came next, and I knew I wouldn't give up.

So I prayed to God to help me as I took up the task of discovering the cause of my condition. This became a personal mission, and by Wednesday night I had begun diligently researching medical conditions with symptoms similar to mine. I couldn't sleep, anyway, because I was worried about being shocked again, and I was using relaxation techniques to calm myself and slow my heart rate. Focusing on finding the diagnosis to my condition provided relief from fear. Cardiac sarcoidosis kept popping up in the research articles I saw, and it seemed to match exactly with the symptoms I had been experiencing. I wondered how my doctors did not come to the same realization given my age, symptoms, and overall medical history, and since cardiac sarcoidosis is listed as a differential diagnosis to be considered.

I have a documented disability with the VA of circulatory and neurological issues due to toxic chemical exposure, which had left me with neurological and circulatory damage, and my symptoms fit perfectly with cardiac sarcoidosis. I became certain I was dealing with cardiac sarcoidosis and probably sarcoidosis in other organs too. I felt some relief and hoped that it might be medically managed if treatment was administered as soon as possible. I felt relief that the cause of my heart failures might have been discovered. However, I'm ashamed to say that my pride swelled in knowing that I was able to determine my diagnosis when my team of doctors could not. I failed to give some of the credit to God, because he was with me during my investigation, and to be honest, it was because of him that I was able to stay focused.

When I asked for God to help me, I received feelings of peace instead of anger. I felt empathy for my cardiology team rather than blame. I realized this knowledge did not come from within me. God led me to those articles about other soldiers with Gulf War illness who were struggling with sarcoidosis and other autoimmune diseases after toxic chemical exposure. And the research articles began to pile up. Autoimmune diseases appeared to be my era's version of Agent Orange that Vietnam veterans suffer from, and just like the Vietnam era Veterans toxic chemicals are the cause of much suffering. I knew I needed support and understanding from others, and I had to stop blaming my medical team and feeling contempt for them. I finally realized why I had always felt good helping other people: it allows you to step outside of your problems and become a force of good for another person. So now I knew I needed to put my anger aside and work compassionately with my doctors to assess the probability of the sarcoidosis diagnosis and proceed with testing for it.

The next day, I showed them all of the research I had found. I told my doctors that since the cause of my condition was unknown, I wanted them to test me for sarcoidosis. They had done CT scans back in August, and they felt my chest, lungs, and lymph nodes were clear of any sign of sarcoids at that time. They said that the scans taken were not the best tests for sarcoids, and they admitted that they had not considered sarcoids as a differential diagnosis. Once they reviewed the research I had given them, and because of how persistent I was about testing for sarcoids and how certain I was that sarcoidosis was the right diagnosis, they ordered the additional testing.

For the first time, they candidly admitted that they did not have any experience with sarcoidosis and were uncertain how to treat it. They explained that most people with cardiac sarcoidosis die from cardiac sudden death, with diagnosis being made during autopsy. So they brought in an excellent pulmonology and critical care team to run biopsies in an attempt to isolate tissue with sarcoid granulomas present and other tests to rule out additional illnesses. A new CT scan and MRI showed a high level of sarcoids in my lungs, lymph nodes, and other organs that was not present four months ago. I began to wonder if all the shocks might have caused my sarcoids to spread at an incredible rate, because those shocks at the very least increased my stress levels, and there was inflammation from the trauma.

Over the next couple of days, I endured many more tests and biopsy surgeries than I care to recount. I was constantly in pain, but I seemed to breeze through the tests because it felt like we were starting to zero in on a positive diagnosis and not just waiting for more problems to arise. I grew more optimistic and hopeful that sarcoidosis would be determined to be the cause of my symptoms, and then we could actually begin to treat my condition. I knew I couldn't control the outcome, but at least now I could focus on steps that could lead to a better outcome.

As the results came back, the evidence pointed to sarcoidosis, but my doctors were unable to isolate specific sarcoid tissue from the biopsies performed, leaving them without a positive diagnosis. They explained that a biopsy only captures a very small target area, and if that small biopsy does not contain the sarcoids, then they have to try another area. However, they were able to rule out every other cause for the CT scans and MRIs positive results and found no other possibilities for my symptoms. They also were able to eliminate all other differential diagnoses and proved no other conditions were present in my heart, lungs, lymph nodes, and nervous system. They planned to continue biopsies in other organs but wanted to try the less invasive ones first.

Tina sent Ann and Joey to her family's cabin up north for Christmas in an attempt to shield them somewhat from this newest hospitalization. The entire family was already so traumatized from the events I endured over the past four months; they didn't need any more. I looked as if I was only hanging on by a thread, and truthfully, I think the kids were all surprised that I hadn't died, but I was stubbornly fighting for life. Tina didn't feel the kids should see this one, as I looked so tired and weak, and she later said she thought I was about to die. I looked like death warmed over, and the shadow of death itself seemed to loom over me, despite my positive outlook and hope for a treatable diagnosis.

Elijah refused to leave me. He wanted to be with me every minute, and so he came with Mom every day to see me. He even took naps in my hospital bed with me. He told me how worried he was when he got home from school on Monday and found out I was in the hospital again. Having no idea about what was going on had scared him. He said he was worried I was going to die without him saying goodbye. He said his sister wanted to stay but went with my youngest so he wouldn't feel so alone; Tina's family planned a lot of activities to keep their minds off the situation. They didn't tell my youngest about the seriousness of my situation to avoid adding more stress on him. Ann made me a lot of personalized get well cards and several times told me how I was the best dad a kid could have. She told me to keep fighting because she loved me and needed me. This meant a lot to me, especially coming from a teenager who was typically very moody. So I thought I should at least make it through this, because of that kind of outpouring of love.

At this point, I realized I'd have to stay in the hospital over Christmas and then would be transported to Mayo Clinic soon after. When I realized how long I would be away from my family, I felt my heart was literally and figuratively breaking. This separation did not make any sense to me, as the doctors were unable to do anything different for me while in the hospital than they could if I were to go home to recover. My doctors were barely visiting me anyway, as most of the hospital was operating on a holiday schedule. I pushed for release by Christmas Eve and told my doctors that I'd come back if my condition became unstable again and that I would follow up with Mayo first thing on Monday morning. I was firm that if they didn't release me, I would leave on my own and that if I was going to die, at least it would be with my family.

My children were very upset and concerned that I would die, so I knew that coming home and celebrating Christmas with the family would help them to recover from the trauma more quickly. I knew I could endure the pain and discomfort if it put their minds at ease. They had just barely started to feel more comfortable with the progress they thought I was making prior to the Cleveland trip. Tina and I had kept the fact that my health had been severely declining from them, to avoid adding to the anxiety they were already feeling, but this incident brought back all of their fears and intense sadness, especially being so close to Christmas. So I decided I would get out by Christmas Eve, no matter what it would take. I felt that if I was going to die, it shouldn't happen alone in the hospital, where I wouldn't even have the chance to say goodbye to my family. Almost all of the doctors were gone with their families, anyway, celebrating the holiday.

This turned out to not be a problem, as my cardiology team was fairly disengaged with my treatment at this point and only visited a couple of times to chart my progress. The hospitalists were all too willing to discharge me as soon as possible, because they had no clue about how to proceed in my treatment. So when the hospital could not make arrangements for my transfer to Mayo Clinic until well after Christmas, my cardiology team signed off on my discharge papers, releasing me from the hospital on Christmas Eve per my request. The only stipulation was that my heart had to be reasonably stable for a couple of days prior, and I was given specific instructions for when I should return to the hospital.

My critical care team stepped up in a big way and arranged for pulmonology and critical care appointments. They scheduled pulmonary function (PF) tests on December 27 and scheduled a lung biopsy to check for sarcoids on January 4. My pulmonologist told me that he believed I had sarcoids from my symptoms; my test results seemed to be textbook for the disease. These appointments required that I cancel my Mayo Clinic evaluation. I felt too sore, tired, and physically exhausted to make the trip for three full days of exstensive appointments, especially since sarcoids would cause a different course of action than the previously scheduled tests were to focus on. I was certain that I'd be diagnosed with cardiac sarcoidosis, and when I called Mayo Clinic they agreed that ruling in or out sarcoidosis would be critical to determining the best course of action. They encouraged me to continue with the testing, as they also felt sarcoidosis was likely. They assured me that once we knew more they would reschedule the necessary appointments for me without delay. I wasn't even a patient yet, and Mayo Clinic had already taken more of an interest in my health than my actual doctors—with the exception of the critical care team—were currently showing.

CHAPTER 14

The lung biopsy that my critical care pulmonologist scheduled for January 4 consisted of sticking a needle through my chest into my lung and extracting tissue for analysis. This was reported to be a fairly safe procedure, but some risks are associated with it. I was disappointed that we had to go to this option to get a suitable sample to make the sarcoidosis diagnosis, but I was ready to do whatever was necessary. When I arrived at the hospital for the lung biopsy, I met with the surgeon prior to the procedure; he had thoroughly reviewed my medical record and felt confident he could get the results necessary to make the diagnosis through the lymph nodes in my neck, which would be less invasive and easier to make an immediate diagnosis, as long as I was willing to take the chance of having to have both done if the lymph nodes were inconclusive.

I thanked God because I knew he made this game time decision possible, probably to spare me additional pain and suffering that the lung biopsy would cause. The surgeon warned me that if he was unable to obtain a definitive sample, he would still need to do the lung biopsy, but I was certain this would be successful.

The lymph node biopsy was completed, and the initial results had clear sarcoid granulomas; we would not need to go through with the lung biopsy. I was ecstatic because the lung biopsy had more risks and is more difficult to assess. The biopsy tissue is very small, so if the tissue extracted does not contain sarcoids, it obviously would not help to diagnose. Two days later, the official results of the biopsy made it definitive that I had cardiac, lung, lymph node, and nerve sarcoidosis. The formal diagnosis was made. So on January 6, I began treatment of daily doses of prednisone.

I felt certain God would aid the medication in its effectiveness to break down and remove the sarcoids, restoring me to health. I finally felt some relief from the hopelessness, fear, and anxiety I had been feeling. My anger at my situation began to lose its power over me, now that I had some hope that I might live. I finally had something to actively fight against; this was a gift from God.

My physical and mental health had continued to decline since August 27, and I was now looking forward to improvement through treatment of the sarcoids. At times, I allowed my fear to trigger false confidence to protect myself from the feelings of anxiety and panic. I failed to fully credit God with helping me to get to the point that the diagnosis could be made, but I was making clear and steady progress in my relationship. I now could clearly recognize his work getting me to this point. I still hoped to feel closer to God and was learning to trust him and his plans more fully. For now, I felt some hope and peace in the fact that all I had been through may now be successfully treated, pushing the sarcoids into remission. I knew I would continue to fight this thing, and with God's help, I truly believed I would be victorious. The only thing that caused me fear was that despite his will to heal me, I might be shocked again before the treatment for sarcoids took full effect.

CHAPTER 15

Sunday, January 15, 2017, was another significant turning point in my life. It had only been twenty-two days since being released from the hospital on Christmas Eve, and it was only 142 days since this whole nightmare began. On Thursday, January 12, I started to feel a significant increase in my arrhythmias. I called my device clinic to alert my doctor, but they said my reports looked fine and I did not need to come in. I felt horrible and sick all weekend. This was terribly reminiscent of the last time I had heart failure on December 19, not too many days ago.

Then it happened: I started to go into a fast heart rate with sustained ventricular tachycardia just before midnight on January 15. This time, the tachycardia was just below the threshold settings of my device. It was so agonizing to just have to sit and wait, wondering if I would receive a shock at any moment. My head was spinning, and I couldn't catch my breath. I felt like I would pass out at any moment; my heart was pounding so hard for so long that the pain rapidly increased to an overwhelming level.

My heart was pounding as if I was being punched in the chest over and over, without a break; breathing was as difficult as if I had a vacuum sucking the air out of my lungs as fast as I was trying to gasp it in. Sadly, this had become an all-too-familiar experience for me over these last 142 days. After an hour without improvement and no response from the cardiac team, Tina decided to call 911. The first responders were many of the same ones from the first heart failure event back in August. It was nice to see them, given the situation. My condition was severe, but they tried to keep me calm and kept the mood light and encouraging until the paramedics arrived. They told Tina and I how the last time they were at our house, after I received the first cardioversion, I had asked for another "jump." I only wanted to ease my pain, but now it provided a humorous story, because as they reported, no one had ever asked for that before. I guess when you're in pain, you'll even take more pain in the hope of finding some relief. This just proves that not all pain is bad; sometimes, pain can make you stronger.

They told Tina how tough I was and that I'd make it through this one too. Their kind and calm demeanor made her feel better. They said they were amazed at my resiliency and strength, for remaining calm and positive during this current situation. In truth, I felt like I was going to die, and I was worried. I just didn't want to appear weak and afraid in front of other people or to worry Tina even more than she already was.

Something was different this time; I could sense it in my body and almost feel it in the air. It was like death was looming over me, ready to take me at any moment. The air around me was charged with a strange electricity. I was definitely not as optimistic as I appeared. I realized this time it was very serious, even more serious than the others, possibly due to the continuous strain on my body. I was still weak from the last time I was in the hospital with heart failure and exhausted from my daily battle with the sarcoids. Now I feared being shocked to death, as the arrhythmias were so prolonged. The months of pain and suffering had really taken a toll on me, both physically and mentally, and I no longer felt the same fighting spirit I used to have. I felt like I was stuck in the middle of a minefield, and every step may lead to a devastating explosion. I needed to draw upon my strength, but it seemed as if my reserves were empty.

It was icy on the roads that night, and when the paramedics arrived, I was immediately taken to the ambulance; IVs were administered and medications given to try to stabilize my heart rate. It was the same process as the other times, and I was becoming a pro at assisting the paramedics. I was transported to the emergency room as quickly and safely as possible, because the concern was that I would go into cardiac arrest at any moment. Once I arrived at the hospital, I was brought into the same critical care room as before. I was starting to feel all too familiar with this scene, and I could recite the process the doctors would take to lower my heart rate.

There in that room, they attempted to stabilize my heart rhythm with more medication and placed the AED's sticky pads on my chest and back, in case they needed to bypass my defibrillator. My arrhythmias were constant and just below the therapy threshold of my device. I felt like being shocked was now inevitable; the doctors were seriously considering initiating a shock manually, because my prolonged elevated heart rate could cause me to go into cardiac arrest.

I spent the next six hours in the emergency room, desperately fighting for my life and praying for Jesus to spare me for a little longer. It's funny how at the end, nothing but time seems to matter, as it grows short. I knew I was dying, and time was growing short. I really wasn't ready to leave my kids; I knew how sad they would be and how hard it would be for Tina to support the family. I had plenty of time to think of many sins I had committed and had apologized, knowing I didn't want to come face to face with God without apologizing in life first. It's amazing how genuinely remorseful I became when death was so close. I was unable to convince myself of all the good things I had done, which I usually would put forth as evidence of my worthiness as a good person. I don't think people are really able to lie to themselves when death closes in.

I used to think deathbed confessions were pathetic, desperate attempts to plead for forgiveness. I now realize that when you're facing death, you do appreciate how wrong your actions have been. I wished I had done things differently. I was afraid because I knew I had no choice in living or dying. I wanted to keep fighting, but I felt weak and helpless. I knew that death was a very serious possibility at any moment, and I was scared. For all my life, I believed I had a fighting chance in any situation, but now I knew I was at the mercy of my fate. In fact, I felt I was more likely to die than to live. I was not thinking about what comes next, but I was focused on all that I would be losing and everything I had not yet accomplished.

After fighting for my life for about six hours, the ER staff felt I was stable enough for transport, and I was moved to the ICU. I was somewhat relieved that things looked to be improving, but I still felt like death was hovering over me. Shortly after I was transferred to the ICU, the ventricular tachycardia started up again.

I was still hooked up to the same IV medications, so the nurses contacted the on-call cardiac doctor and emergency room doctors to tell them the arrhythmias had returned, despite the medications. I was in a lot of pain and exhausted due to the long fight in the ER, but they were unable to give me anything for the pain due to the danger of cardiac arrest. I didn't mind because I did not want to have my will to fight dulled by medications. They attempted to treat the ventricular tachycardia more aggressively but were concerned that I was seriously weakened from the length of the battle thus far. My heart began to decline even more severely, and the ventricular tachycardia increased over the next half-hour. I heard the doctors tell the nurses that they were concerned I may go into cardiac arrest at any moment. They said I wasn't responding to the medications and to prepare for the possibility of sudden death. I was still more afraid of being electrocuted by my defibrillator than anything else, but then my attention was drawn to a Crucifix on the wall directly in front of me. Ironically, it was the only place I was able to look.

I was now too weak and exhausted to move my head, even if I had wanted to, and the Crucifix was drawing me to it. It almost seemed as if it was communicating with some part of my soul. I soon realized this was a loving reminder of Jesus's sacrifice and the strength he would provide us when we most need it. I took the opportunity to pray for forgiveness of my sins of pride, selfishness, anger, and fear, as I felt death creeping ever closer. I asked God for the faith to trust him fully, and I also asked him to give me the strength and the courage to endure the pain, no matter what outcome was in store for me. I asked Jesus to remove my fear of dying, because I was alone in that bed, and then I felt the fear begin to melt away. I wasn't even afraid of the shocks anymore; I just didn't care.

Then around 7:30 a.m., I started to experience respiratory failure and felt like I was suffocating. My organs began to shut down, a code blue was called, and the room was filled with emergency medical personnel.

By the time I began to experience the respiratory and organ failure, the doctors and nurses had already been working on me steadily, but then the entire crisis team seemed to be in a frantic rush. When they began trying to distract me with personal questions about me, information that they already had, I knew the situation was getting worse, and the end was soon to come. I often used this same technique to distract angry and violent patients in order to change their thinking patterns. I would ask what their favorite movie was or some other random and unexpected question. Either they would think of the answer or ask what it mattered, but at least we would be discussing something other than what was bothering them. This proved to be effective, even if it was only for a few moments. Distracting my patients this way would give me a window of opportunity to calm the situation down by changing the way they were thinking. Clearly, the doctors didn't want me to do what I was doing, which must have seemed like I was giving up the fight to live.

The crisis team's entrance reminded me of the scene from *The Wizard of Oz* when the flying monkeys came storming into the haunted woods to take Dorothy, wreaking havoc on her friends. The room grew dark, just like those haunted woods, and the medical team's movements were like a blur in my peripheral vision. First, the monkeys come swooping down through the trees out of nowhere and struck terror into the group. Then they surround the Scarecrow and began ripping him apart. This was the feeling I was having, totally helpless and overwhelmed, feeling as if my body was being ripped apart and pulled in every direction. When the crisis team came into my room, they seemed to rush through the doorway, and about twenty medical personal were soon in the room. I was completely surrounded. There was a lot of yelling and movement all over the room. I felt more like the Scarecrow as they were moving all my limbs about and strapping me down to the table. They weren't ripping me apart, but it sure felt like it on the outside and the inside.

This was a chaotic situation, even though each person knew what they were supposed to do. For me, it was quite overwhelming; I had no clue what was going on, but knew I was going to die soon. Waiting for my death in this way was a very surreal experience. I was completely helpless and could do nothing to stop death, even if I had wanted to. My desire to cling to life was diminishing with each moment, and I almost welcomed the relief that it would provide. The hurried commotion and noises were so stressful and disorientating; the only thing that kept me calm was the Crucifix. I had the feeling that Jesus was very close to me now and felt a source of strength I had not previously recognized.

I could hear them readying the AED and shouting that they were losing me. Fear still tried to dominate my thoughts, but I found it easier to push the fear aside at this point. From here on, time seemed to fly by like the last remaining grains of sand in an hourglass. I felt I did not have much time, as I could hear and see the medical staff's futile efforts to save me. Suddenly, a feeling came over me, and I became aware that I definitely was going to die. I had felt like I was going to die for the last three months, but now, I knew it was definitely coming in a short time. If they could not stop the ventricular tachycardia, I knew I would die very soon, but now I actually knew I was going to die, no matter what.

The doctors were yelling for me to keep my eyes open and to keep answering the personal questions; they asked my name, address, what I do for my profession, and so on. They were constantly asking me to keep my eyes open and to stay with them. I knew that keeping my eyes open would give me strength to fight for life, but I also knew it would only extend my life for a few painful and lonely moments.

During all of this, I could feel that Jesus was with me in that room. It's hard to explain this sensation, other than it was a very tangible feeling, like when having a nightmare as a child and one of your parents comes in and hugs you. Jesus was somewhere close by, perhaps even hugging me, and knowing this encouraged me to at least fight off the fear of my approaching death.

I didn't want to keep answering the questions the doctors were asking because it was distracting me from praying and watching death complete its work. This experience was so strange; knowing that death was going to take me soon and I would see God was exhilarating and terrifying at the same time. I had never felt Jesus closer than I did at that moment. I was thankful for his presence and really can't imagine going through this without him. I knew fear was trying to prevent my prayers and distract me so death could blindside me, but I decided I was going to spend these last few moments in life with Jesus. Despite the uncertainty of what was going to happen and what was yet to come, I felt a sense of calm come over me, and I was able to fight off the fear that accompanied death.

The pain was intense and excruciating, and I was growing exhausted. My heart wasn't responding to the medications to slow its beating, and my implanted defibrillator was not being triggered to initiate therapy now that I needed it. So the doctors began to use the AED to shock me, as my breathing became more labored. My organs were failing since my heart had been working too hard for too long, but not pumping enough blood to sustain them. The first shock ripped through my body like a violent dropkick to the chest. I was strapped to the bed to prevent the shocks from throwing me off. I felt my strength drain even further; the shock seemed to steal my strength and had no effect on my heart rate. Then another vicious shock was delivered, with the same results. I was not able to keep track of how many shocks I received, but none of them helped. The shocks were unable to slow my heart rate, and the end was closing in on me.

The force from the AED would have jolted me off the table, so it was a good thing the nurses had strapped me down first, but at that point, I didn't even care. I no longer feared the shocks. Surprisingly, I was no longer afraid of death, either; giving myself over to God's will released me from all negativity and eliminated my fears. When the AED fired and the pain didn't stop, I closed my eyes again and debating whether to open them again and fight or just let go. I felt my will to fight evaporate when they were unable to stabilize my arrhythmia with the AED shocks. My vitals continued to drop. I was no longer afraid of the shocks, as the pain I was already feeling was overwhelming, and the AED barely produced any sensation in my body at all, despite the severe jolt it produced. The room was so chaotic that I felt more at peace with my eyes closed, blocking the scene out of my mind, but I couldn't eliminate the noise, which was overwhelming.

After I prayed, I felt I had been forgiven. I didn't feel scared that my sins would prevent me from finding peace. I no longer felt hypocritical in asking for mercy and forgiveness while I was dying. In fact, it was just the opposite: I finally felt free, as if I actually was released from all my wrongs. I knew that Jesus would take care of me, and I understood the pain and suffering of my life had a greater purpose; they were not punishments for some wrong I had committed. I knew with the medications and the AED not stopping the arrhythmias, I could not survive much longer. I was becoming more comfortable and less anxious about my approaching death. In fact, I just wanted the pain, the chaos, and especially the noise to stop. I wanted to move on to the next life and to be free from all of this.

The doctors were shouting my name, calling, "Are you there?"

I answered yes, but the effort to speak was so difficult at this point and the experience was now so painful that I no longer wanted to acknowledge them.

The doctor replied, "I need you to open your eyes," but my response was, "I don't want to open my eyes."

It took a lot of effort for me to talk; I only wanted to pray during those last moments. I didn't want to talk or open my eyes any longer, in part because I didn't like what I was seeing and hearing. It was just too chaotic. I only wanted to pray and talk to Jesus while I died. I just wanted to experience my death peacefully. I only wished my family was there so I could say goodbye. Talking and opening my eyes only brought into view the desperate situation I was currently in; the conclusion was already obvious to me.

At this point, I knew I was moments from death. I could feel death closing in all around me. I was not going to last much longer. During the past few months, and in my last hours, I had been truly afraid and beaten by this world and the pain it had brought me, but now, I had some peace from accepting my fate. After hearing the doctors yelling my name and imploring me to open my eyes, I decided to just lie there and die peacefully. I stopped talking to the doctors and focused only on praying to Jesus. If I could have had them plug my ears, it would have been perfect, because the sounds of that room were so terrible. Despite this chaos, it was surprisingly easy to talk with Jesus as I lie there dying.

The last thing I managed to do in this life involved me giving up on a fight. This was the first time in my entire life I can remember backing down or giving up on anything. Ironically, it was the fight for my life. I was usually like a dog on a bone, relentless and tenacious in a fight. I never cared about the consequences to myself; I only cared about the successful outcome of reaching my goal. I did love my life and those in it. I had always felt I had lived life to the fullest, but now I felt like I could have done more with my life. I felt that I had more to offer to the world, and my full potential would now never be realized. It would be wasted. It was strange, though, because at the same time, I felt better after I relinquished my need to control the situation and turned my trust over to God. I felt free from something that had constrained me my whole life. The illusion of control seemed to keep me stuck in appearances, not based on the things that are truly important to my soul and my life to come.

I began to realize that every accomplishment or good deed I had ever done had been more for me than for the sake of doing good alone or for those who benefited from them. Somehow, the good I had done gave me the positive reinforcement of being a good person. However, all my courage, bravery, and honor in life were not of much importance, because they were not perfectly aligned with compassion toward others. Truthfully, I did them for my own benefit. I had always liked being seen as brave, courageous, and honorable. It isn't like I was wrong for this; they are honorable traits, but it's just that I was not being as noble as I had thought. I realized now that I would not be able to do anything to change my life or to glorify Jesus any further. I really wanted to show gratitude to him for never leaving my side during this ordeal; somehow, this made me feel sad, disloyal, and dishonorable, and yet I also felt forgiven and free. I learned that Jesus is a true friend, loyal and caring until the very end, despite how I treated him in life. He even made my death more tolerable. It was surprisingly peaceful, considering the pain I was in and the chaos I was enduring.

CHAPTER 16

My Visit to Heaven

In the light of Heaven, the worst suffering on earth, a life full
of the most atrocious tortures on earth, will be seen to be no
more serious than one night in an inconvenient hotel.
—Mother Theresa

I felt myself continuing to physically drift off, slowly fading in my ability and desire to endure this fight for life. I couldn't shut down mentally and just drift off to sleep, as I hoped I'd be able to, because even worse than the pain was that I couldn't block out the noise and chaos of the hospital room. As thoughts (mostly regrets) kept racing through my head, I began to long for the pain to finally end. It seemed as if I was being attacked by these thoughts and they were trying to convince me I would not be accepted by God, but I could feel his presence with me the whole time, and his mercy and forgiveness were apparent.

As the doctors were talking, it sounded as if their voices were now moving away from me and coming from within a tunnel or a deep well. My eyes were still shut, because the blackness was more appealing than the view of the hospital room. The pain was intolerable, and every second felt like torture. I began to wonder how much longer I'd have to endure this. I was still concerned with what was going to happen next in the death process. I thought about how sad it would be to never see my family again and that I did not even have a chance to say goodbye, but

I prayed for God to watch over Tina and kids in my absence and to help them through this.

I then I felt my body die. It was just like that. A split-second, and I went from being alive to being dead. I quickly realized that I never had any power over my life and even less control over my time with it. When death came, it felt like everything physical was abruptly shut off. In an instant, everything sensory was simply gone, like someone just hit the switch, and everything as I knew it physically was gone. The chaos was gone. The sound was gone. Taste was gone. Feeling was gone, thankfully, because I had been hurting so badly. The change in perception was drastic.

However, when my body died, my mind kept going, never stopping for even a second. I was conscious of everything that was happening to me, even how death felt. In fact, my consciousness grew immensely, and I had a more precise sense of awareness. The difference being that I was processing everything at a faster, clearer level of functioning. I knew I was still me, and I realized I never lost conscious thought for one instant, but I knew that I had died. It was incredible to go from chaos to death and to feel my consciousness grow in a split-second and to have all the negativity gone in that same span of time.

I know I cannot accurately explain the feeling of dying, but I'm going to try. It is obviously so hard to explain death to anyone who has not had this experience, because it was unlike any other life experience. People typically experience death only once; it's usually the last experience we have. My physical existence, with my physical body, did stop, and all my human senses were gone instantly, but without a doubt, my spiritual existence continued. This new existence is beyond human understanding and makes any attempt at explanation difficult. It is even difficult for me to understand, and I experienced it. The knowledge of what had just happened with my physical body was very apparent to me but was not distressing. I wasn't scared at all. What was continuing to happen to my soul was strange but somehow familiar and also extremely exciting at the same time.

As I realized that I had just died and was now unencumbered by the limitations my physical body had presented, everything became clearer to me. I felt my soul leave my body with a sudden shake and a quick pop, then everything abruptly became soundless and dark. It was like a blender suddenly being shut off. All of the noise, vibration, and chaos of life suddenly stopped; the relief was extreme and sudden. I was quickly ejected from my body. I immediately welcomed the silence after experiencing the chaos of the hospital room for so long. The pop seemed to break my soul free from the confines of my physical body and shook me free from the physical world. It was the strangest feeling I had ever experienced. I can only liken this experience to being born backwards, but it is probably more like when the soul is entering the human body at conception (but of course I don't remember that experience, and this is only speculation).

My eyes were closed when I died, and it was dark prior to death, but it felt as if the shake and pop pulled me backwards, through and out of my physical body into a more serene and secure space and state of being. I instantly opened my eyes; it had now become tremendously dark and intensely quiet, and I immediately knew I had died. At the very moment of death, I was aware I had died; it did not have to be announced or proven to me. There was no confusion; it was obvious that I had just died. I simply knew my death as the obvious next step for my life, like waking up from a dream, the difference being I felt more alive now than I ever had in life.

I cannot stress enough that I never lost consciousness. I maintained continual awareness in my mind of what had happened and what was currently taking place. This was exciting to me because I knew I died, and I wasn't afraid. In fact, I was extremely interested in what was happening. As a psychology geek, it was obvious to me that I had died due to the extreme changes I could perceive consciously, psychologically, and physically, but I remained the same mentally. I was now experiencing all my faculties and senses in a fully enhanced way. A profound feeling of amazement overcame me as I realized that I never lost consciousness, knowing that I was not dreaming and I could determine the precise moment I died and what it had felt like. I was also amazed with knowing what was happening to me now and that I was fully experiencing all the changes that had taken place and everything that was currently happening.

I was clearly and distinctly aware of my death, except now I had absolutely none of the fear, sadness, anger, or any other negative emotion experienced in life. Those emotions were gone the instant I had died, and because the peace I was experiencing was so powerful, I could not have recalled them even if I wanted to. I realized I had died and was somewhere else in that same instant. I went from the hospital room to a completely unfamiliar dimension. When I first opened my eyes, I saw a vast darkness, a space bigger and more expansive than anything I'd ever seen before or even imagined. It eclipsed the depths of the Grand Canyon and exceeded the span of the ocean. It resembled pictures I've seen of outer space in our universe, except it was absent of stars, planets, or other sources of light of any kind. It was just a vast, empty black space, but somehow, I could see its vastness.

At first, it seemed black, as if I had no sight at all, and when I say it was quiet, I mean it was quieter than anything you can imagine. It was completely absent of all sound. It seemed as if all the sound had been turned off instantaneously. It was absent of any sound at all, so that I could not even hear that constant ringing in my ears from tinnitus, which I have had since the military. It was very relaxing and peaceful, like being in a sensory deprivation chamber. I could also no longer feel the overwhelming pain or the intense fear. I could not even feel the sadness from just moments ago; in fact, those emotions were replaced by an overwhelming sense of peace, love, and joy. These new feelings were intensely flooding into me and overtaking every part of my soul. One second, I could hear the doctors and the commotion of the hospital, but in the very next moment, even the same second, with no point of division, I could not hear anything at all, and I now had these profound changes in my emotions. It was so amazing.

At this point, I was no longer afraid of death, and I knew I had just died. It seems that after it happens, it's easy to just move past it and accept the new situation. I still had the memory of my death fresh on my mind; interestingly, all the other memories of my life were also present, simultaneously. I kept thinking about how I never had a break in my conscious awareness even when I died and was astounded by the experience of my high level of conscious activity and awareness. It was expanding so that all my memories were now present and accessible at the same time. I knew I had moved from the physical realm of life into a new spiritual realm that magnified everything from senses to emotions to thoughts. Yet it was all so positive, and I felt fantastic. I was excited to see what would come next.

As I stared into the blackness, I had this thought: *Well, this can't be it.* I momentarily considered this conundrum and then asked myself how death could lead to nothing but this dark space and yet still be overflowing with positive feelings. I also asked myself how everything else had drastically improved. I knew there must be more to the afterlife than staring off into some sort of black emptiness. It had to be more than some eternal nothingness, especially with this profound physical, emotional, and mental acuity infiltrating my entire being and maintaining the fullness of my consciousness. I could also still sense that Jesus was somewhere nearby, and I realized he had never left me. He seemed to be the source of the peace, love, and joy I was experiencing, because it felt like it had in the hospital room, only more magnified, powerful, and penetrating. Somehow, I was more completely connected to him, and I knew he never left me for an instant. I then began to wonder how I could see the depth of the darkness if there was not a source of light. I wondered if I could now see in the dark too.

I didn't feel as if being a certain religion was a requirement to experience this, but I simultaneously felt Jesus was an obvious truth in this place, I was certain that he loved me and was somewhere very close. I did not see any signs of religion, and it was never brought up. Of course, religious implications could be argued both ways. I do have a religion, and I believe being a Christian made it easier for me to accept all that was happening, but I am not sure that everyone doesn't get to enter the same way and then still has a choice to accept the truth or reject it. The thing I am completely certain of is that only peace, love, and compassion seemed to matter here. Love and mercy were what this place seemed to be all about, and I feel like anyone, even a nonbeliever, would most likely feel this closeness too, repent, and choose to stay.

I felt that they would certainly feel the love and peace, and I think they might have a final chance to experience God's love and mercy and then still be able to attain eternal peace. I don't know this for sure, because I never asked, and I went into it loving Jesus. And of course, I would still suggest everyone to at least make a deathbed confession or, better yet, to not risk it that long, because I'm not sure what happens if you die instantly and haven't accepted Jesus previously. I never asked about the particular rules to get here, but I can tell you that the love was so powerful, it is hard to imagine anyone not having a chance to change when they felt it pouring into their soul.

It felt like God loves so deeply that even nonbelievers would not stay stuck in their resistance, and it seemed like our human desire to control could cause us to remain in the dark tunnel or enter further into the dark vastness in which we originally arrive. It also seemed that his vast love and mercy would allow for the opposite decision. I was aware that I loved God fully, and I had no doubts about his existence, but I felt like I had the freedom to choose to stay in the dark, alone, forever, if I had wanted to. I cannot say what was in the darkness or about whatever else lay beyond. However, I can tell you I wanted nothing more than to be with God and away from the dark. I also knew God was very near, and my desire was drawing me to him. I was so certain of it that I began looking around for him.

I profoundly enjoyed the immediate change in my emotions upon arriving here. How could I not relish the change, as I was now filled with peace, love, and joy, and these emotions were magnified, unlike anything I had ever felt before. I felt more energized and stronger than I was seconds before, as I was dying, and I felt even more vitality than I had ever felt in my life. I no longer felt like I was going to die; in fact, I actually felt immortal now, unlike I had imagined I was when I was younger. I had never felt peace this intensely at any other point in my life, nor do I believe I ever will (at least not until I die the next time).

The peace, love, and joy I felt are not easy to describe with our limited human vocabulary, nor can the knowledge and understanding I suddenly possessed be even remotely translated. I cannot accurately explain the intensity and purity of those feelings because no comparison in life currently exists. So please bear with me as I attempt to describe this unexplainable experience with as much precision as I possibly can, given my limitations. Just remember that this was the most profound experience I ever had and the most intense feelings I've ever experienced.

I could clearly remember every detail of my life, all at the same time, without distraction, and the multitude of memories did not cause me any confusion to see them all at once. At the same time, I could focus on any one event in full detail, like when I was remembering every detail of my death moments before. I remembered my death without the process being unfocused or distorted by the other memories I saw. My consciousness was totally uninterrupted, and I was creating new memories of the situation as it was occurring. In life, I was limited to choosing one thing to focus on at a time; perhaps there were times I was able to multitask a couple of insignificant topics simultaneously, but now, I had endless possibilities.

It's crazy for me to think about it now, but my entire life unfolded for me; all my memories were present and accessible simultaneously, while my current situation was also being experienced and committed to memory. I was able to control each thought, idea, or memory individually and in full detail, while remembering all the others and still taking in new information. This increased mental acuity was totally amazing. I had never imagined that this kind of clarity was possible, and I have never had anything close to it since. Explaining this concept in human terms is difficult, even though I experienced it and still remember how I felt. I think I could really explain my mental abilities accurately if I still had them, but unfortunately, I do not. I only wish now that I had known I was going to come back, so I would know how to explain it.

The vast expanse I first found myself in after dying was completely black. Well, after I questioned how that space could not be all there was to the afterlife, I realized I could actually see the emptiness and the vastness of the dark space. It was obvious that some source of light was shining into the dark space from behind me. I knew I did not have my physical body, because I felt so light and free, without any pain at all. I do not know if I cast a shadow or not, but I did not see one. I did feel like I was still in some kind of physical form, though, like I had some physical boundaries, but I could not see any part of my body. I did feel that my innermost being, my soul, was contained in some sort of a body with borders but no limitations. I wasn't familiar with this type of body, and its boundaries did not seem at all constraining or restrictive. However, this body did feel absolutely natural and more comfortable than my human body could have ever been, especially when I contrasted the condition I had just left my human body into what I felt now. This was great.

I don't recall hearing, smelling, feeling, or touching anything or needing to. My vision seemed to dominate my experience, and it was coming from within this spiritual body that was engulfed in positively the most perfect peace and love, which was so pure and strong. I'm not sure if I could use my other senses or not, because I didn't try them. I didn't feel like I lacked my other senses, and it did feel like everything was so amplified, but I had complete awareness, so no additional sensory input was necessary, unless I chose to use them. My eyesight was profoundly improved, and I was infatuated with understanding how my new visual functions worked, but at the same time, I didn't feel limited to only my eyesight. My knowledge, thought process, and emotional feelings were also so vastly improved, and they were so impressive and fun to explore that I never felt the need to check my other senses as closely as I was inspecting these. I was having a blast.

I was not too hot or too cold, hungry or thirsty, and my new spiritual form felt so comfortable and natural. I wondered how I could have tolerated my previous physical body with all its physical pain, emotional distress, and mental weaknesses. How could I have stood the desires and temptations leading to so many negative emotions, which in turn kept the cycle of ever-present fear revolving like a merry-go-round with no way off? I remember thinking I had never felt so wonderful, so free, and I reveled in it like a child escaping its parent's grasp at bedtime, extending playtime a little longer. I began to focus even more on my eyesight and was intrigued that I could see more clearly, farther, and in more directions than can be explained because again, there are no adequate human words to describe what I was experiencing. I think saying I had 360 degree vision comes close to describing it, but I could also see through and around objects. I could choose to not see through one object and look at another behind it while still seeing the first one simultaneously. It was like I could just visualize everything, no matter where or how it was positioned. Nothing was hidden from my view.

While I was longing to see God and be with him, my awareness was suddenly attracted to the bright light that was shining from directly behind me and flooding into the darkness. This light was what allowed me to see into the darkness all along. It felt like I was standing in the middle of a dark country road, on a pitch-black night, when I suddenly realized a semitruck is approaching from behind me, illuminating the darkness. Yet I knew this light had always been visible, as it had always illuminated the pitch-black darkness, providing me a view of its true vastness that I could not have seen otherwise. I was not yet fully used to my new visual capabilities or enhanced thought process, but I could control my enhanced vision and see the depth of the dark vastness in front of me and fully see the light behind me simultaneously, engulfing me completely and penetrating the void as well.

When I turned my visual focus to the right to see the light behind me, it felt as if I was being directed by an internal magnetic pull, drawing me toward the light. As my focus rotated, I could still see the darkness. I realized that the glowing light was brighter than I anything I had ever seen before and was shining through every inch of space. It was truly amazing and even overwhelming as I realized that this light was the source of the love and peace.

The light was so bright, I really have nothing to compare it with in the frame of reference of our physical world. Even to say that the sun did not compare to the brightness of the light doesn't really do justice in explaining just how bright the light actually was. Sure, the light was brighter than the sun, but it was so much brighter that I cannot explain it with justice. The light was such a far distance off through the dark tunnel where I currently was, but it was clear to me that I wanted to be right there with the light. I could sense that the peace, love, and joy were emanating directly from this light source, and I knew my soul belonged there with the light. I was irresistibly drawn to the light but still free to do what I wished.

Effortlessly, I began to head toward the light, but I arrived much more quickly than I had expected, given how far away I was from the light initially. The light had appeared so far away from me that I don't know of a measurement I could use to describe the distance. I was so far away, like the distance when looking at the moon, and I was amazed at how rapidly I reached the light. I must have traveled at close to a million miles per second. So you can see why these new experiences are so hard to explain. Physical laws of distance and speed in which I could travel didn't seem to apply here. Interestingly, as I rapidly approached the magnificent light, I did not feel any wind or inertia to provide evidence that I was moving as fast as I appeared to. The usual laws of physics did not seem to apply.

This moment was so strange because I had wanted to go to the light and simply arrived there, almost instantly. However, at the same time, I had a clear memory of taking every step as I was approaching the light through this dark tunnel. There was no blur in my vision as each step flew by rapidly; I could recognize each and every detail of every one of the steps through the tunnel.

When I arrived at the light, it was like I had stepped out of a cave or a tunnel of complete darkness, and I was now standing before this enormously awesome, wondrous, and radiantly brilliant light. It positively and powerfully emitted love and peace, which was intensely palpable and seemed to shoot directly into my soul, filling me with peace, love, and joy. The light penetrated throughout my entire being, filling me with an energy and excitement like nothing I've ever felt before. My spirit felt on fire with joy. Imagine the best day of your life; you know which one. It's the one you had the most fun and most positive emotions of your lifetime. I can safely and easily say that day doesn't even come close to the positive feelings I was receiving from just being near this light. I truly felt as though I had been designed to be here with this light, as if I belonged to it. I loved the feeling as it resonated throughout my soul.

It's truly difficult to describe anything I felt or saw. I say difficult not because it is hazy in my memory, but because describing the infinite in finite terms, as a temporary being as I am, and saddled with my limited vocabulary, is impossible. Try to describe the love you feel for someone another person dislikes very much, and then add the fact that the other person is unfamiliar with the whole concept of love. This is what it feels like to describe the wonders of heaven and the magnitude of God's love.

Now to describe this light as enormous would not adequately define its immensity, because the light even surpassed the vastness of the black void in which I first arrived. It was millions of times brighter, or even perhaps it was magnified by a number I cannot possibly grasp; it is too large to explain and too complex to comprehend. The light stretched all the way up as far as I could see and as far as I could see down, and it seemed endless from right to left. Keep in mind that I could see really far now, and perhaps I had no limits to my vision. Imagine being an ant and standing before the Great Wall of China, and you'll have a pretty good idea of how I felt standing before this massive and awe-inspiring light.

I was able to recognize this light to be endless right away. My vision attempted to reach the end of its border; however, it just kept going. The light seemed to take up every single bit of space, everywhere I looked. The gigantic hole of blackness from which I had just emerged did not even compare with the vast size of this dazzling and majestic light, as the light even penetrated into it. It was light like no human can understand, and it's too difficult to describe the magnificence of that light adequately without some sort of frame of reference. A feeling and personal presence emanated from it, which was even more profound than my extreme inability to express it. The best analogy I can come up with is that this light would have swallowed the sun, just like a searchlight swallowing the light from a thin candle.

I can still remember the complete and astonishing magnificence of the light. I also remember what it was actually like standing before it. I have no words that can even come close to describe the light, but it felt more intense and comforting than sitting in the warm morning sun. It's difficult to explain because my human physical and mental orientations prevent me from fully understanding and describing the magnitude of the light. Perhaps its magnificence is not intended to be fully described but only experienced at death. Add to that all the diversions and distractions life constantly assaults our consciousness with, and you start to see my dilemma. When I was standing before the light, I felt only the love I had been experiencing since I arrived emanating from it directly. Now none of the pain or anxiety life often brings were even remotely present, and only peace circulated through my soul.

Standing before the light, my complete attention was drawn to it, as if the light was all that mattered; it made my existence meaningful. I can assure you that no light exists like this in the natural world, and yet, it was more than a light; that's the only way I have to describe it. There is no object of similar size; the entire universe as we know it could easily have fit into the light. This was not only a light, but it was so much more. I am limited in how far I can see back in our world, but when I was in front of the light, I could see farther than the distance from Earth to Pluto, with full clarity, but the light extended way beyond that distance. It is impossible for me to define what it is like to see that far; it must be experienced to fully understand what I am trying to express. I was instantly aware of how small and inconsequential I was physically, compared to the light, and while I was in awe of the light and realized my insignificance next to it, I was not afraid. In fact, I was in love with the feeling of love generated by the light.

The light was also pure white and brighter than anything I had ever seen before. No special effects that I've ever seen could compare with it, nor can any words that I possess begin to define the brilliance of the light. It made the sun look like a distant star, small, dull, and dismal, but the light had no blemishes or imperfections. It was perfectly white, but surprisingly, it didn't hurt my eyes. In fact, I remember thinking, *I cannot believe I can I look at this light without it hurting my eyes.* Instead, I felt a strong connection to the light and felt that I never wanted to stop looking at it or standing near it. It was more striking than the brightest, thickest bolt of lightning, flashing against the blackest of nights. The light was more substantial and palpable than a thunderclap if the lightning had struck the ground right next to me. The light also emanated power through the air around me and into my being, and the power pulsated love and peace. I felt safe, secure, and comforted.

The light consumed everything, especially my soul, and you know what? It felt marvelous. I felt totally loved by this light; it radiated peace, joy, acceptance, and of course love, more powerfully than the concussion from a powerful explosion. When my defibrillator radiated its painful shocks throughout my body, that was nothing compared with the pulsating love I was now feeling.

Obviously, the light did not cause me any discomfort or fear, and it actually eliminated all negative emotions I had. It blew my mind and filled my soul completely with love and a sense of peace and well-being. I realize I keep stating how impressive the light was, but I truly couldn't stop marveling at it. I was consistently amazed by the power of the light more every second I was with it. I am still amazed by it. The light seemed to hum, a sound that accompanied the light emanating love. It sounded like a meditation mantra, om, and reverberated peace and relaxation of all anxieties.

I once again thought, *I cannot believe this light doesn't hurt my eyes,* and I was curious how the light could be alive and love me so much. It seemed to be pure energy but more alive than anything I have ever experienced.

At that moment, I realized the light was God, and yet I also realized I had already known that it was God from the moment I saw the splendor of the light, even from when I first entered this place. It was really fun to experiment with my expanded mental clarity; God was more familiar to me than anything else in my life. It felt as if I had always known God, and I could recognize how he was with me throughout my life. Talk about déjà vu, but it was as if I had known God from the moment I was conceived; I felt he was present with me throughout my life, but my choices in life had created a barrier between us. Those choices and life's other distractions caused me to forget my true familiarity with God, but the love I was now experiencing reminded me. Now I remembered once again, and this too amazed me, because I realized we are all of God, actually created from his energy, and we belong with him. That is our natural state of being and why I felt so safe and comfortable. I could truly be myself, and I felt unconditional love.

Suddenly, but almost instinctively, I was completely aware that God (the light) was telling me that I could come through the light, that if I wanted, I could enter into him and pass into heaven. I felt this overwhelming peace, love, joy, happiness, tranquility, and serenity just being near God's light. It was like being wrapped in a blanket straight out of the dryer, so warm and comfortable, but when I entered the light, I felt myself absorbing and changing into these qualities I felt coming from God.

I remember thinking, if I can even call it thinking, because it was more like I had one specific thought at that moment, yet this thought was one among all the other thoughts, memories, and ideas I've ever experienced in my life. All were present at the same time, but I was focused on this particular one. This type of thinking was ever present, and it too was amazing. The thought I had was that I now had a greater awareness and greater control over the thoughts I chose to focus on. All of this occurred without losing sight of all the other thoughts as they replayed through my mind simultaneously, but it still allowed me to focus on one thought more comprehensively. This made thinking really fun. I also thought, *How can I think about so many things at once and with such clarity and not become confused or distracted?* I actually enjoyed every minute.

I suddenly understood that I had no desire to control the situation or my actions. I simply wanted to be near God and to be with him, always connected in this way. I lost my illusions of control and realized God has control over my life. I fully trusted him and wanted to do whatever he desired because of his profound love for me. If God asked me to crawl through a sewer full of excrement, I would have been happy to do so just because of the wonderful feelings I had simply being with God. I still had my full free will, but I didn't feel like I wanted anything except whatever would please God. Playing the game of life, impressing others, ambition, greed, and unneeded desires are all a waste of time. Freedom from all these is just on the other side of the walls we build around ourselves. The freedom can be found here in life, with work and faith, but is instantly achieved in heaven. I felt totally safe and completely loved, like being in the arms of your parents as a child, only more intensely.

I had never felt anything as powerful and perfect as this love, and the deeper I went into God's light, the more intense the power of that love became. Even my love for my own children did not compare to the feeling of love I was receiving from God. I can tell you that I love my children a lot; in fact, there is nothing in life I love more than my children. As I started to go through the light, I felt overwhelmed by the changes that began to happen in my spirit. Everything lifted in me, even more than when I first arrived, and my own feelings of love and peace became so much stronger and so pure. I could feel the love and peace emanating from me now too, as if I was a conduit of God's love. I had no negative emotions at all and held no grudges from life. Additionally, I did not have any desire to reexamine any of the suffering of my personal life. I was full of forgiveness for every insult I ever experienced. I actually felt pure mercy and compassion for the first time in my life. My recent death and all the events leading up to it even seemed to be a joyous occasion, now that I was filled with this love and peace.

I had to die physically to be free from life's entrapments. For the first time in my life, I was totally free from the bondage of the prison of my own creation. This was a prison built with bricks of resentment, fear, and selfishness. I never really thought they had much of an impact on my life, but in reality, those strong walls prevented me from achieving the freedom and happiness that only God can provide. It was like the fulfillment of my soul's purpose; something I had been lacking all my life was now completed. It was like the vast, dark, empty void I first arrived in was that part of my human soul that only God understood and could fill. My void was full of love and peace; it was now flowing through me and back out from me, leaving that space fully illuminated. It is true that God's love is endless and all powerful. I only had to stop resisting it.

I was still amazed at how I had full awareness of my past life; I never lost consciousness or awareness of what was happening and was making new memories at the same time. Specifically, I was amazed that I could readily recall every moment of my recent death, the transition into the dark void, and my entire life without a lapse in my memory. It was like an amped-up computer, popping up new tabs with every experience or event from my life. It was like I entered into myself and had full control over my entire mind. I was processing these new experiences while simultaneously recalling all my life experiences at the same moment.

The pain and loss I had endured during life didn't matter now; instead, each moment was replaced with an enormous amount of love that more than compensated for any of my life's inconsequential sufferings. In fact, my sufferings now seemed to make more sense than I ever realized. I knew that being in this place right now was all that mattered to my soul, and I felt that attaining this should be my only ambition. It was all that ever mattered and all that will ever matter. I also knew that I was created to be here in this place. For the first time in my life, I felt as if I really knew who I was, and I was totally content with myself. I discarded all the masks that I've ever worn in life. I was happier and had more joy than I ever experienced before. I was totally energized with excitement and felt there was no limit to my happiness.

I have never been comfortable sleeping anywhere but in my own bed. However, I now felt truly at home; my earthly home couldn't compare with it. Imagine being away from home in a hotel; it's noisy, the bed feels different, the room is not organized the way you're used to, and you don't want to use the shower. It was different in heaven; I felt I had just left the hotel and returned home. It was a total fulfillment of my soul, and I felt a rejuvenating effect come over my whole being.

I no longer feared death, and I found it ironic that although I was physically dead, I felt more spiritually alive than ever before. I also wondered how I could have feared this while I was dying. The feelings I now had were so wonderful that I could only remember that I had feared death prior to coming here, but I could not recall the actual feeling of fear. It's like trying to remember how unsteady and nervous you were when learning to drive, but twenty years later, you don't even think much about it; you just drive.

I thought about how I had been so afraid in those moments prior to my death, and now I wondered why I felt that way; I knew that God's love had been with me throughout my life. I went skydiving once, and the concept of jumping out of a plane is only scary as you anticipate the jump. I felt anxiety prior to actually jumping, but once I had committed to the jump and made that leap, it was too late to turn around, so I settled in and enjoyed the experience. I have always liked exciting experiences and really thrived on the adrenaline. Death, however, provided me more joy, excitement, and freedom from fear than I have ever known. I didn't have to overcome my fears; they simply were gone. It was like taking that leap from the plane; my anxiety disappeared. I was filled with joy and excitement once the illusion of control had been overcome. The need to control has caused more anxiety to my human soul than any real danger ever has; I realized I've never really had control of how events unfolded in my life. I simply made choices in certain situations, and then I've had the natural consequences that followed.

I'm not sure how long I spent basking in God's light, taking in his love as I was walking through him, but it felt so wonderful. I know I could have been happy if I stayed there forever. I cannot describe how time was experienced in heaven. It is kind of like summer vacation as a child. One day, you leave school for the last time that year, and before you know it, you're already going back. You know you had a lot of fun over the summer, but it's already gone; it was like waiting for Christmas to arrive. My modest human means of understanding and limited vocabulary again make it impossible to describe such a complex concept. For example, I was dead for just ten minutes in earthly time, but this near-death experience (NDE) seemed to last a lot longer than ten minutes, due to all I was doing, but it also seemed to flash by in an instant. I think that this uncertainty of time was in part due to my ability to conceive all time, past, present, and future, simultaneously. As this experience became part of my memory, it was stored along with all the other memories of my life, although this experience felt more natural, real, and more familiar than any I had ever had before. My time in heaven is still the most significant and poignant experience of my entire life. I often feel like life is simply a dream and that I am waiting to die again and wake up, so I can be back in heaven.

God's light was so thick and so dense that I could feel the warmth and pressure. It was like being wrapped in a warm blanket after coming in from a cold and windy day. It was so full of living emotion, but yet I could travel though it so effortlessly, as if I was a part of it. I was filled so full of love and with so much joy; I am truly overwhelmed as I sit here trying to explain it now. It seemed to me as if I was part of the light and had always been part of it. The light felt like the original energy source of all creation; all things came into being directly from it. I don't know what kind of body I had at this time, as I did not try to look, but it was clear to me that it was fully connected and united with God in and through this light. I understood that all human beings, every single one, were made for this connection with God.

I remember thinking at this point, *I want to see Jesus.* This thought was standing out in my mind, above all other thoughts. As I thought this, I only had to move forward ever so slightly, and I was stepping out of the light. Once I stepped through the light, I entered into a room that was even more enormous than the entirety of the universe. It was much greater in size than the black vastness I found myself in when I originally arrived, and it was wholly engulfed by the light of God. This room was completely encapsulated and protected by God's radiant and wondrous light; this seemed to be the entrance to heaven. This was just a glimpse into the wonders that heaven held, and still, this was not even close to the whole of what was awaiting in the fullness of heaven. It was like a large reception room, and it seemed as if everything had been in place, just waiting for me to arrive, but I instinctively knew that there was so much more to come, and yet this had already exceeded my expectations of what heaven was like. When I was a child, my grandpa told me heaven is full of singing and dancing; I thought that sounded terrible because I didn't like singing and dancing at all. I didn't see any singing or dancing, but I wouldn't have minded because of how wonderful it felt to be surrounded by God's love.

The atmosphere in that room had properties that I cannot begin to describe. I know I keep having difficulty describing what I was seeing and experiencing in heaven, but to put it into perspective, I'll ask you to try explaining the beauty of a rainbow to someone who is blind and cannot comprehend the concept of colors, let alone the beauty and wonder of a rainbow, and then add to it that this is your first time seeing anything at all. Any description given could not fully explain the depths of the rainbow. A rainbow can only be appreciated through our personally experiencing it; no words can do it justice. If I was a person who was born blind, gained vision long enough to see a rainbow, and then lost my eyesight again, and then I was given the task to explain that rainbow to another blind person, that's how I feel now trying to explain heaven and all of the wonderful feelings I experienced there.

The atmosphere was green, pink, and several other colors I had never seen before, all dancing and sparkling together with the glow of radiant light bursting through every single particle. The atmosphere was unlike anything I'd ever seen or felt before, and it also seemed to be positively charged with love and peace. It was absolutely alive and filled with love for me. Imagine that: The atmosphere was actually alive and cared immensely about me. The atmosphere appeared to be filled with a communal love and peace; it served as a direct connection between God and me and everything else there in heaven. In this room, nothing appeared hidden, and I had a complete understanding of all things in existence. A full awareness of the mysteries of heaven were shared with me, without anything being withheld from me.

There were other beings around me there too, an enormous crowd of them gathered into this room, which I instinctively knew was only a small part of the heavenly inhabitants. Communication with God and these other beings seemed to pass through the atmosphere and create a communal consciousness among all of us. This atmosphere and the collective communal consciousness connected all of us beings directly to God and Jesus. I started to suspect that it was the Holy Spirit. All the beings present were welcoming me at once, but I could also hear each one individually. This was all happening without confusion, as my mind could process all this information instantaneously. I did not try to recognize any of the other people; I am not really sure why I didn't even try, other than having a strong desire to see Jesus. I did, however, feel connected to them all, and I know I knew them, even if I had not met them during my life. I could feel their thoughts, my own thoughts, and memories from my life and theirs, with an abundance of new ideas as they surfaced all at once. I was still without any distractions, confusion, or misunderstandings. I had complete clarity. Everything in my consciousness was perfectly ordered. I could control every thought, memory, or idea I ever had, all at one time, while still focusing on the conversations of the other beings and my own thought process about what was going on at that moment. It was totally awesome. Now, it's overwhelming to contemplate, with my limited level of consciousness and the distractions that accompany us in this life.

The other beings had more of a spiritual form than a physical form, but they seemed to be shaped like a human torso, and they had clear outlines. They presented as a physical form with the impression of glittering and sparkling light bursting through them. They shone with brilliant light that sparkled throughout their bodies, and then that light combined with the light shining throughout the entire expanse of that enormous room. It was obvious to me that the light of God emanated throughout everything in heaven, including all the inhabitants. The dazzling light seemed to be positively charged within them; each of their individual cells seemed constantly in motion, bursting light out into space and connecting with each other within the glow of God's love. I did not focus on any particular being because I was so entirely obsessed with seeing Jesus. I thought once again, *Where is Jesus?*

I could feel that he was somewhere nearby, even closer now than I had felt before, and I desperately wanted to see him. Truthfully, I really wanted to see his face, in part because I needed to see if it really looked like what I imagined it did throughout my life. I also wanted to see the face of the one who loved my soul enough to die for it and then, after seeing all the horrible things I did in my life, still would stay with me and, upon my death, bring me into a place as wonderful as heaven, instead of leaving me in that dark void or seeing me off to an even worse place.

Suddenly, my attention was drawn toward the brightest being present; I was immediately attracted to its brilliant illumination. It was like I was zeroing in on a military target, except I was using love, and I could feel the love emanating from him into my soul and out to all the other beings present. My heart seemed to beat in sync with his; I was fully connected to him. I became fixated, as if I was in a trance of love, and I knew this being loved me. I did not want to break my gaze or look away, even for a second. As I looked at this being, I was clearly aware that it was Jesus. I was so sure of it and without any question of it. I began trying to get his attention and have him acknowledge me. My curiosity was at its maximum. His light shone on me so brightly; I felt his love so fully and knew him immediately. I cannot describe how it felt to feel the love of Jesus like this, face to face. It was simply too strong, pure, and unconditional to put into words. I can tell you that today, I still miss his love and presence with all my heart. I know his love has not diminished in the least, and it is only my inability to perceive it that prevents me from feeling it fully here on earth. As I recognized Jesus, I felt a huge weight leaving me. I felt that I was so much closer to God and connected to the love of heaven than before.

Jesus was so bright; illuminated beams of sparkling light exploded from him into the room and beyond. Those beams of light exploded so forcefully that his love could be felt everywhere. I initially couldn't distinguish his face because it shone with the most brilliant light, far exceeding all other lights. Still, I desperately wanted to see him, so I tried to force my vision to bring his face into focus. I thought, *I have to see your face, Jesus; this is the only thing that my heart wants.*

His face started moving and coming together, like when you focus on an object and it begins to split, and you see two images, except this was in reverse. I started to distinguish his features. A flood of excitement came over me as Jesus's face came into focus. I could see all the other beings clearly now too, but I focused my attention on Jesus. Every one of the other beings around the room became visible at the same time. No one was hidden from my view, even if they were behind other beings or located very far away in the enormous room.

I could not stop focusing on Jesus. Now that I could see him face to face, I had no desire to look around the room; it was not important for me to focus on the other beings at that moment. I did not specifically recognize or communicate with anyone I loved in life, but I knew they were there. I could feel them near me and hear them in my mind, but my attention remained on Jesus. I just didn't have any individual conversations with them. When I saw that I was looking at the face of Jesus, I immediately realized his face was full of love, and I saw that he was smiling directly at me. His face was filled with such care and kindness, and I wanted to continue looking at him. I loved looking at him, and I must say that having him look at me was the highlight of my life. Seriously, imagine someone looking at you, and it being such an exhilarating feeling that all the pleasures of life can't compare with that gaze. Seeing Jesus made dying worthwhile.

I recognized Jesus instinctively; it was as if I had seen his face before. But at precisely the moment I was seeing his face, I began to forget it. Can you imagine seeing something and forgetting it at that very same moment? It was as if when my eyes looked on his face, my brain could not record the image to memory. Somehow, my mind was blocked from recording this image, while my eyes could see him, and I was still aware that I was seeing him. I could see what he looked like, and I will never forget that he was smiling and full of love for me. Even though I cannot recall his features, I knew he was looking lovingly at me at the same time.

Instead of including a lot of verses from the Bible, I wanted to keep my story strictly about what I saw and experienced. But since the concept of seeing Jesus's face and, at the same time, not remembering it is so complex that I have trouble contemplating it, I felt I needed to add this verse after I came upon it and related strongly with it:

"Moses said, 'Please show me your glory.' And he [God] said, 'I will make all my goodness pass before you and will proclaim before you my name "The Lord." And I will be gracious to whom I will be gracious and will show mercy on whom I will show mercy. But you cannot see my face, for man shall not see me and live'" (Exodus 33:18-20 ESV).

His face was so bright, and he radiated love and peace all over the room and onto all the beings present, even into them and into the atmosphere surrounding us all. He was directly connected to God's light. The image of his face seemed to go past my eyes without being recorded in my memory, I would never be able to bear to be apart from him again, or my frail human heart would actually explode if I was not directly in his love and peace. This seemed a necessary protection for my own safety.

"There He was transfigured before them. His face shone like the sun, and His clothes became as white as the light" (Matthew 17:2).

"Who is this who shines like the dawn, as fair as the moon, as bright as the sun, as majestic as the stars in procession?" (Song of Solomon 6:10).

"In his right hand he held seven stars, from his mouth came a sharp two-edged sword, and his face was like the sun shining in full strength" (Revelation 1:16 ESV).

Then I started to wonder why I had died. I was not upset about dying; it was only that I recalled a memory from when I was about seven years old, following the funeral of my great-grandmother. She was one of the sweetest and most beloved people I've ever known. After seeing the weeping of my other family members at the sight of her motionless body, I felt I never wanted my death to cause such pain anytime soon. I remember praying for a long life, and then I suddenly felt a strong feeling of peace, love, and calm come over me, as if the prayer was being granted.

As I recalled this memory, I also recognized the feeling I had all those years ago was very similar to the feelings I was now experiencing in heaven. However, those feelings I experienced as a child were not even close to the intensity I was currently experiencing. As I was thinking about this moment of my life, Jesus made me aware that he also recalled that prayer and that he had indeed granted my request that night. He also let me know that he would still honor my request, if that was the choice I wanted to make now. I could choose to stay in heaven, or I could have additional time in life.

I knew Jesus was telling me that I could either stay in heaven or go back to my life. He made it clear that either choice was acceptable and in line with his will. He made sure I knew that neither choice was better than the other. He also made it clear that he was going to let me make the decision for myself. I felt so much support and love from the other beings present while I was making my decision. They were all perfectly united with what Jesus was offering me, and while they were happier being in heaven, they understood if I desired to go back and would welcome me back once again at a later time. The unity of this heavenly crowd filled the atmosphere, and yet there was no sound, just a deep understanding and cooperative consciousness. At the same time, there were distinct, separate, and distinguishable messages encouraging me to make whatever choice I wanted to make.

The feeling of being in heaven was so wonderful and awe-inspiring that it was hard to even think about going back to my life. When I first tried to think of a reason, I focused on my children and wife, because family has always been the most important thing in my life. I tried to think how hard it would be for them and imagined distressful situations that might befall them so that I could find a feeling of concern for them not being able to protect themselves. Since I could only feel peace, love, joy, and perfection in heaven, it was impossible to feel any trepidation, knowing that heaven would also be awaiting them. I realized all the suffering I had endured in life or the sufferings anyone else would go through, including my family, were of no consequence once they reached heaven.

My sufferings had been turned into advantages and opportunities to develop compassion for others and destroy my personal selfishness. Now my traumatic sufferings seemed merely an inconvenience that brought me newfound strengths. I found trying to make this decision was more about trying to find a reason to rationalize going back to life and leaving the wonders of heaven. Even when I thought about leaving my kids without a father and Tina without a husband, I understood that Jesus would always care for them, as he had always cared for me. He showed me that I did not need to be concerned about their well-being if I stayed in heaven. He showed me how the paradise of heaven that I was experiencing now would be awaiting them, and he would replace any of their sufferings with the unimaginable peace, love, and joy that I was now experiencing when their time came. I started to realize that choosing to go back must be for a greater purpose than just trying to return to my life as I had previously lived it, although that would be the obvious result.

Then all at once, yet still in an orderly manner, not at all chaotic, I understood that these other people had left loved ones behind too. Some left children, spouses, or other family members, while others left various other people they cared about. They all told me that now in heaven, they appreciated how God takes all their pain away and replaces it with even stronger feeling of love and peace. I knew this was true, too, as I experienced it immediately upon arrival. Many of these people were telling me how they endured great loss, pain, sufferings, sicknesses, and sadness during their lives, but in the end, they all recognized that everything had worked out to God's great plan. They all could see the wisdom of God's plan now.

They told me how God had used those sufferings to create good in their lives and the lives of others; they always felt extreme joy now that they were in heaven. I realized that now for me, too, as I could see the good that had come from the times I suffered. No matter what I had suffered during my life, it was of no concern to me now; in fact, my sufferings were replaced with exceedingly high levels peace, love, and joy. All sufferings were replaced with and I was infused in the very love of heaven. Suffering was no longer haunting my psyche and had instead become a badge of honor and filled me with greater depths of love and compassion.

I had just died a physically painful and emotionally draining death after a relentless battle with multisystem sarcoidosis, with extreme cardiac sarcoidosis for five months. It had been 142 days to be exact, but now I felt it had all been worthwhile. I certainly did not feel like that prior to coming to heaven. I could feel myself dying over this time, and there was nothing I could do to stop it. I felt it was worthwhile not just because I got to see heaven and directly feel the love of God, but ultimately, the sufferings I had in life created a closer relationship between God and me. My fight held no negative associations for me any longer, and in fact, it seemed totally worthwhile. Death was worthwhile.

The message was crystal clear, that the pains that happen during our time on earth will be no concern to us while we are basking in the love of heaven's eternal life; instead, they be seen as blessings. I knew this was true, as I felt no pain, anxiety, or sadness over my recent death. Those emotions, previously present prior to my death, had been eliminated from my mind, and I was unable to recall any negative emotions or thoughts. I could see they were only temporary illusions, but now they were to be seen for what they really were. I could feel how my soul was made to be here, and that void in my soul, the longing for significance and acceptance, was no longer present. It had been filled up completely by God's unconditional love. I really felt like I belonged here and nowhere else. So how could I choose to go back to my life full of pain and inevitable suffering? This decision was clearly going to be difficult.

It was great to hear from the others how families will be joyously reunited in heaven; pain and fear will be removed, and there was no sadness, selfishness, jealousy, or anger. I felt this decision I was being allowed to make was also part of God's plan, and all things in life that I may suffer if I chose to go back would only be used to later receive the permeating feelings of love and peace to an even more profoundly magnificent effect, and they would connect me more closely with Jesus. All of the pain, sadness, anger, selfishness, and fear I felt were now eliminated, and those memories had become joys as I saw God's plan revealed to me. He showed me how his plan had unfolded, and I immediately realized that as long as I follow his will, he will use the suffering for my good on earth. Then he showed me how he will replace the suffering with an overabundant amount of joy in heaven.

I understood that only God can save anyone, and that it was his right as the creator. I was only responsible for my actions and choices in life, not the outcomes. I had previously thought too highly of my own abilities and strengths to direct myself during my life and obtain the outcomes I had wanted. I always believed I had a duty to protect those I love and to achieve my goals through my own efforts. I did not need assistance from anyone else, as I explained in my introduction. I immediately realized how wrong I was and how this mentality affected others, myself and especially Jesus, during my life. It negatively affected my relationships with others more than I could ever imagine. I realized that I couldn't bear the pain a second longer prior to my death, and I did not have the strength to continue to fight for my life.

And in the end, prior to my death, I had just given up to bring it all to a final close. I saw how weak and fragile I really was in comparison to the certitude of death. Jesus once again came to me in my time of need and brought me out safely. I realize I was not as strong as I had always thought I was during my life, but I also realized that God is so much stronger, kinder, and more loving than I had ever thought.

As I then contemplated God's will and my weaknesses, such as pride, selfishness, and anger, I realized the only possible reason to return to my life again was to try to eliminate these faults and replace them with love, mercy, compassion, and kindness toward others. They had to be continuously flowing from the love and peace I was learning here in heaven and used to bring others to the awareness of what really lies in store after death. I knew going back for this reason was to help turn souls for Jesus and to glorify him as I now fully realized he deserves, because of his great love. The way he wants to be honored is by our helping others to feel his love through the compassion we show them. That really isn't a difficult concept to understand.

I realized that I was being taught that showing love and kindness to others is the only way we have to honor God. It is the only way to show our love and appreciation for Jesus, as our showing God's love to others is a direct reflection our understanding of how he loves us. The compassion we show to others brings mercy on our souls and covers our immoral actions and unethical behaviors better than any penance. It is good to aim at accomplishing this, because God doesn't want to lose a single soul, and so we must participate in that objective in order to offer him anything of value. He loves us all, each and every person, and wants the same love to flow from us to the world for everyone to see.

I knew that if I went back, the fear, sadness, and pain I had left would return immediately, and I also knew that because of the limitations that physical life places on our minds, it would not be easy to endure, especially after I had experienced this place. I also knew my suffering would now be better understood but still painful and challenging. I felt I could endure it, having experienced this overwhelming love and peace, but I knew the pain would also be worse for me considering the trauma I had suffered during my death, and so what I would return to would be horrific. This experience of true love and pure peace restored my courage to endure the pain and renewed a sense of purpose for my life, despite my disabilities. I saw how real strength didn't come of my own physical capacity and abilities, but it came directly through the fulfillment of my connection with Jesus. I was not sure how I would serve God when I returned, but I knew that only my effort to do so mattered, and he would lead me to the opportunities. I just needed to remain open to his promptings, and his will would show me the way to the outcomes.

I was given a long time to think about my decision; it wasn't easy, because heaven is so splendid and beyond my ability to explain. I took my time to enjoy the glory of heaven, but it was so wonderful that now looking at the experience, it felt like only a moment. It just flew by.

This was certainly the biggest, most important, and most difficult decision of my life. I knew Jesus was encouraging me to share this love with others if I chose to go back, but he also wanted me to be with him in paradise. He wanted me to show compassion to others, but he also was encouraging me to stay with him and enjoy paradise, if I preferred to do so. I wondered if I really wanted to leave this wonderful feeling for the pain and misery awaiting me in the hospital room. I knew it would be okay if I stayed; I would be reunited with my family again. I now understand that I spent some of my life looking for God, but he spent my entire life showing himself to me, planning for me to be with him. His love is immeasurable, and the impact of his love on my soul is what made it so difficult to choose to leave.

Finally, Jesus asked me to give him my decision, and he reassured me again that whatever I decided, I should not second-guess myself, as it would be used within God's will either way. I knew it would be a sacrifice and a great challenge to go back to the pain and confusion of life, but I was no longer afraid. It would not be an easy task to manage my human body, full of emotions like fear, selfishness, anxiety, anger, and sadness, all of which were absent here and replaced by perfect love and peace. It was inevitable that I'd struggle with these at times again, but I felt that I would better understand them now and more easily overcome them now that I had this new knowledge of their impermanence.

However, I was fully aware that any future sufferings in life would not match the glory awaiting me in heaven at my next death. I also knew that I could endure the suffering that I would return to for the glory waiting for me, if I serve God well through loving others. I would no longer consider my life to be my own, but instead, I looked at it as belonging directly to Jesus. I would allow him to completely use my life as an instrument to save others and encourage them as he sees fit. I felt a strong desire to do this to glorify him and to reciprocate the love he has for me as best I could. I wanted to go back and show love for others and do good work, despite the longing I was feeling to be close to Jesus and to stay in heaven. I was already beginning to feel a growing love for Jesus that seemed to consume my soul, and I was certain life would never have a chance of breaking it.

As I stood there before Jesus in the midst of heaven, I discovered that I wasn't afraid of death any longer. I knew I could face it again. How could

I be afraid now that I saw what was awaiting us? There is no reason to be afraid of death, because heaven is even greater than I ever imagined it would be. So I thought if I went back, there would not be any anxiety or suffering that life could throw at me now to hurt me; nothing could shake me or my faithfulness after seeing heaven. I learned that there is something deep inside of me that cannot be defeated any longer, and the world cannot begin to touch it. That dark void is now full of light. This new resiliency comes directly from this very real connection to God, and we all can achieve it whether we have seen heaven or not. Now that I have experienced the love and peace of heaven, my resolve and my very soul have been strengthened against the forces of negativity. I am still not sure why I was given this great gift.

I was so elated being in the presence of God, feeling his love in the atmosphere and having it saturating into my very soul. I loved the feeling that my body seemed to pulsate. I knew that with this new reliance on God's love and our connection, I could endure any challenges of life, physical or emotional. Now that heaven's perfection had enhanced my spiritual strength, I knew I would be so much more faithful. So I decided that I would go back and use my time to serve God faithfully with a renewed heart and show more compassion and love to others. I was unconcerned about the condition of my physical heart, or the pain I would return to, because I felt that Jesus had something more profound and important in store for me and a deeper purpose waiting for me if I chose to return to life. I cannot lie: I hoped he was going to remove the sarcoids and then fill up the holes left behind in my heart with his love and grace, but I was willing to accept whatever was to come.

I knew the pain, fear, and sadness I had just left in the world would be waiting for me upon my return, tormenting me and attempting to break me down as soon as I was back. Somehow, I knew that the ultimate evil of the world would try everything to break me. I also knew things would be different for me now, and I welcomed the suffering and pain as a means to become pleasing to God's will, because I could feel his love strengthening me. I chose to pursue the additional opportunities I would have to please Jesus and share his love for me with the entire human race. I wanted to bring more people to his love. I also knew I'd be able to share

God's love with the people I already love, especially with my kids, and this was exciting to me.

I knew that after I returned, the next few years in human life would seem to pass in the blink of an eye as there seemed to be no sense of linear time in heaven. I knew this concept of time was more accurate than what I knew time to be previously, but it is still hard to comprehend from our human understanding. It was amazing in heaven to see how all my memories, like the few that I had described in my introduction and all these new experiences, could be recalled at once, and they could also be focused on individually, as if they had happened only moments ago. It was like having millions of screens replaying various scenes from your life, while you continue to create new memories.

As I prepared to depart, I could feel this enormous pressure coming over me; it was unlike anything I've ever felt before. Of course, the entire time I was there, I felt light or even weightless, with no impediments, but the love and peace I was attempting to leave seemed almost unbearably heavy. It was as if the difficult decision's weight on my mind also transitioned to my physical actions, as I found movement away from God to be nearly impossible. He was like a magnet pulling me back toward him. The love from all of the beings, Jesus, the atmosphere, and God's omnipresence was encircling us all. It seemed charged with love and intermingled with the direct connection to God's ever-present love and peace. Now I was attempting to move away from that connection, and it felt unnatural, like trying to rip your physical body in half, only using the strength you have over your soul.

I felt pressure closing in on me over all points of my body. It was like the feeling you get when you dive into a deep body of water, and the pressure builds up and starts to squeeze, reminding you that you should go no deeper. My soul began to experience some kind of revulsion that resembled pain at the thought of leaving such a wonderful existence. It was the opposite of the pulsating love I felt being near God; it was like being human causes us to block the full effects of his love, and it hurts. As I was getting further from the source of all love, I realized that I needed it, and it felt like I would not be able to live without being in God's presence. It was an excruciating pain, penetrating mentally and physically, unlike anything I had ever felt before. This pain was making it hard to move, as if my internal desire to be with Jesus seemed too strong to overcome, and I wanted to go back, but I couldn't give up now that I had made my choice.

This pain seemed to resonate deep within my soul, and as I forced myself back toward my portal that led to my life, I passed on my return again through the light of God. I felt his love, and it was not diminished, but my knowledge that I was leaving this closeness left me questioning how long I'd be able to hold this feeling before the world would try to swallow me up again. The pain became more severe and my every movement more arduous and labored. It felt as if my feet were fixed in concrete, and the harder I pushed toward the tunnel, the more I felt some force pulling me back from deep within my being. I know this force was the love I had felt from God; he had created a reciprocal love within me, and I was worried that I couldn't live without being near him.

As I then went back into the darkness, every step taking me further from the closeness of heaven, I had to continually focus on how I wanted to spread the love of Jesus and the heaven waiting for us to ease people's fears of death; I needed to share this enlightening certainty I had experienced. I knew that if I didn't, I was certainly going to turn back and stay in heaven. This helped to give me the strength to push on, as God is most deserving of glorification, and if all he wants is to have as many people come to him as possible, then I should do everything I am able to help others to realize his love. So I resolved to make this my life's mission, and I steadily pushed on, despite the pain it caused.

I could see my tunnel as I approached the darkness, and I focused all my intensity on it. I think I could see many more tunnels stacked together like an enormous wall of tunnels, but I can't be sure what they were, as I only focused on mine. It seemed like there were tunnels leading from God directly into the soul of each and every human being, but I instinctively knew which one was mine. Since I did not enter any other tunnel, I don't know if this was what they were for; they kind of reminded me of black holes. As soon as I reentered my tunnel, I felt as if my soul was being pulled back toward God even more forcefully. It was as if my free will was revolting against the decision I had made, choosing to return to life again. I felt as if I only wanted to stay in heaven, that I should stay in heaven, and that this was the only existence I was meant for. Yet I still had a strong motivation to return to life and honor God that kept a fire burning in my soul. It seemed as if my soul knew it was made to be in heaven and nowhere else but that serving God through showing love for other people was the highest purpose I could attain, and I wanted to do more of that. However, it was proving to be the most difficult decision of my life, and it was showing me just how difficult it was through the intense pain I was having as I tried to navigate back home.

I had to constantly remind myself through repetition, almost like I was chanting a mantra, that I would soon be back to heaven, but for now, I had a chance to do even more acts of love. I told myself that it was a worthy decision to honor Jesus for the unmeasurable love I felt from him, and I resolved to not second-guess my decision. I could still feel the enormous love and pure peace of heaven as I traveled down that dark tunnel; it seemed to take forever going in this direction, as my soul tried to pull me back into heaven. So I drew upon all my power to endure the physical and mental pain I was feeling as I departed. That love and peace I gained was filling me with the strength to continue going down that tunnel of darkness, with the intent to serve God back on earth.

At the end of the tunnel, I could see a small circle into our world beginning to form. I still had my spiritual vision, so I could see this circle opening from a very long distance away. I could recognize the hospital room and medical staff, frantically working on me in a desperate attempt to save my life. I knew I was going back and could start to feel my humanness approaching while I was still a far distance from the opening. Traveling through the tunnel from this direction reinforced the impression that I was traveling through a portal from heaven directly back to our world and specifically back into my body. It might be like what being born into the world, as we know the process, would feel like, except it was my soul reentering my body. Perhaps this is what conception feels like. My environment seemed safe and comfortable, and I knew that I would soon be squeezed back into the uncertainty our world produces with its fear, coldness, pain, sadness, and loneliness, regularly experienced in extreme and diverse ways. I realized this was one of God's viewpoints into our lives and that he sees and feels everything along with us. I was encompassed in his light like a spotlight shining on center-stage. He views all of us in the same special way throughout our entire lives.

As I approached, I could see more clearly that at the end of the tunnel was my hospital room. I was viewing it from behind and slightly above my human body's point of view. This must be the vantage point of God when he looks into the portal of every human being. It was actually amazing to see my body and my life from this vantage point.

I could see a big green machine attached to my body doing CPR compressions on my chest; I later learned it was called a Lucas machine. I had never seen one of these machines before and wondered what it was, although it didn't take long to see what it was doing to my body. I later asked the nurse about it, and she was surprised I knew it was used, because they had removed it as soon as my pulse was detected. She said I was not conscious at that point, and my eyes were closed, but I could see the faces of the doctors and nurses as I got closer to the end of the blackness, and I described their positions and activities perfectly.

There was a sense of dread in the room prior to my return; I could hear the doctors calling my name and telling me to come back. Then I heard someone yell out, "We have a pulse; we have him." It seemed as if the entire room breathed a sigh of relief and let out an exhausted cheer. I still wasn't back into my body at this point, but I knew that I now had no choice in returning to heaven and must get back into my body. I braced myself for the impact and onslaught of the pain I was about to experience as I was set to reenter my body.

CHAPTER 17

I instantaneously opened my eyes and gasped for breath, and at that same moment, the portal to heaven abruptly closed up behind me and then forced my soul back into the physical boundaries imposed by my body. That is when I spontaneously revived. I immediately asked the doctors if I had died. I can only explain the return to my body by comparing it to being born, the way we usually think of coming into the world, except I remember it. I felt the same pop and shake that I had earlier felt when I had died again, now as I reentered my body. The doctors confirmed my return to life by yelling to the room, "We got him." It was very strange to feel my soul abruptly snap back into place in reverse process of how it had left my body when I died. I want to emphasize that all of this took place without a break in my consciousness.

I was certain at this point that the portal I had just traveled through was God's direct path from heaven to my body, and I was left with the feeling that I could use it during prayer from now on. I just needed to learn to remove my physical limitations and blocks. I could still sense his love radiating near me as I did before I died. As I had said when I felt my soul reenter my body, it seemed as if heaven's portal closed up behind me, and at the same time, my vision and mental acuity were back to that of my usual human capabilities, just like before my death. I felt that the portal was constantly open from heaven's side, and God's light constantly shone onto and into our souls, but I also felt my body, eyes, and mind simply can't see it without our giving ourselves to God. Perhaps we are blind to heaven's portal without prayer and a relationship with God. Our limitations are probably due to the external and internal worldly distractions and the inconsistencies of our faith. I don't mean this as an insult; I truly want to explain how difficult keeping our faith vibrant can be, given the separation our physical bodies present. Think about this: I was in heaven and saw all that I just explained, and yet the world filled with all of its distractions still provides too much of a challenge for me to see heaven, and I know it's right there, touching me at every moment. I guess this is all part of the test of faith, and we need to cultivate it every chance we get or even better to cultivate it continuously.

The pain, anxiety, and sadness I had previously experienced came rushing back in that instant I returned, just as I thought it would. My physical sensations were flooded with excruciating pain; it was almost unbearable. It was so much more surreal to go from total absence of negative feelings to being inundated with them. Fear, however, was decisively replaced by the lasting euphoria overrunning my soul because of my trip to heaven. Although the pain felt even worse now and was far more intense and penetrating than it had been before my death, it was now easier to handle because I knew how it would be replaced with more than enough love and joy when I returned to heaven next. Perhaps the pain was even worse now because I had endured so much that I had actually died, and during the lifesaving procedures, some of my ribs were broken in the attempt to bring me back to life.

Before I had even regained my breath, I immediately asked the doctors if I had died. They had placed an oxygen mask on me after I died, and it so it was hard for them to hear me, until one came close enough to my mouth to make out my words.

I again struggled to blurt out, "Did I just die?"

He looked me in the eyes and answered, "Yes, you just died."

I really wanted to be assured that I had actually died and did not just have an out-of-body experience. I wanted medical verification, as I remembered my death and everything that transpired after with such clarity that I knew I had to have died. I am sorry to repeat this, but I feel it is very important: I never had a break in my conscious thought during the entirety of this experience. I had fully experienced death and then heaven and finally my return to life. So I wanted medical confirmation that I wasn't in both the physical and spiritual realms at the same time, and I wanted to be sure that my soul had really left my body behind, dead and uninhabited.

I was excited about being alive, not only because I felt God had allowed me to come back, but because he had given me another chance and additional time to do more for him, to raise my family for a little longer, and to try and show his love to others. I kept thinking, *I got to see God. I got to see Jesus. I was in heaven.* I was laughing with a sense of glee when I thought about how I literally walked through God and felt his glory. The doctors and nurses must've thought I had some residual brain damage from being brain-dead for so long. I still have to say, that feeling of love and peace was so much more profound than the devastating pain I felt then.

The pain and fear of the world no longer had power over me. Death certainly did not intimidate me anymore, and I realized I would welcome it as a relief whenever my time comes again. This change in perception about death was life-changing as well, because I knew what was waiting for me. Heaven is truly paradise, unlike anything I had ever imagined. It felt so good when I was dead. I know that sounds weird, but it's the truth.

After 142 days of mental and physical torture, then dying, I finally felt free. In heaven, I felt that all my suffering no longer mattered to me, and neither would any further sufferings I would endure. In fact, I knew now that all future suffering would be worthwhile, especially when I return to heaven again. I knew that I needed to show more love to others for the glory of God; I wanted to do this because of the love I felt from him. The feelings I had carried from the other side provided me so much peace and understanding.

I could have endured anything, even more extreme than the pain I found myself currently in. I don't know how bad that would be or if that was possible, considering the pain I currently had actually caused my death and was so intense that if I hadn't been strengthened by my visit to heaven, I know I would have died from its severity right then. The difference being I was now actually welcoming the time of my death, whenever God may call for it. I saw death as a kindness and a relief from the pain and suffering of this world. However, I was determined to make the most of this second chance and vowed to honor Jesus by trying to win souls with him and by living my life in the best possible way in the process. I keep talking about how I wanted to try to contribute to the winning of souls for him through compassion and love; that is because I now knew he doesn't want to lose a single person.

I also knew it was up to people everywhere to show God's love to each other and to add peace to the world. These were ideals that I had previously found unrealistic or unattainable. There have always been people I had thought were just plain unworthy of kindness, and sometimes, I thought peace was a waste of time, but thanks to my visit to heaven, I am able to tell you I was wrong.

Despite the pain I felt come slamming back at the spontaneous return to my body, my mind was so clear, my thoughts so sharp, focused, and unencumbered by fear and anxiety. I was not disoriented or confused in the least, and I was able to answer questions from the doctors about my address, profession, children, name, and birthdate, quickly and accurately. I was completely oriented to time, place, and person. I knew why I was in the hospital and explained all the events that happened up until my death. I did, however, refrain from discussing what I had just experienced during death; they didn't ask if I went to heaven or what happened when I was dead, for that matter; they were more concerned with running the tests they needed to complete. I wanted to process it on my own first anyway and was content to do so.

The doctors were very concerned about the possibility of brain damage due to the length of time I was dead, so I did not want to further encourage them by talking about a mystical journey until I had time to process my experience myself. After running their tests, they were satisfied that my brain had not sustained any significant trauma and continued on with other tests.

I couldn't account for the duration I was in heaven in human time parameters. This was because the span of time I was out of body seemed to have merely been thirty seconds in earthly time; it was like I was only gone for a moment and then I was back. A simple blink of an eye, but my visit to heaven seemed like quite a long time, perhaps several hours or longer. It was strange for an experience to feel simultaneously seconds and hours and everything in between. From when I died until when I woke up, my human life was unknown to me and completely lost to my consciousness, as I had no awareness of what happened to my body while I was in heaven. The only thing I saw was that Lucas machine on my chest when I returned to life. Otherwise, that time of my life was filled completely with my spiritual experience. Yet while I was in heaven, I definitely seemed to have been there longer than the ten minutes I had been dead on earth, and this was consistent with my conscious awareness. I think it's so cool that there were no gaps in consciousness from dying, touring heaven, and then my return to life. It seemed like I had gained time by dying, because my memory of my experience in heaven expanded my mental time by hours.

I immediately wondered how my death could be the most realistic, wonderful, fulfilling, and extreme experience of my life. How could it be more vivid and intense than the struggle for life that led to my death? How could it be more powerful than my actual death and more extreme than my recovery after coming back from death? How could it be more wonderful than the births of my children? All of these experiences paled in comparison. I wasn't even personally excited about surviving sudden death, because it wasn't due to my personal strength. Remember that I had given up and was too weak to fight any longer. I was excited that I received this wonderful gift from God. Seeing heaven and then coming back was a choice freely given to me by God, and that was the exciting part. My experience during the time I was physically dead seems even more real to me than typing on my computer right now. Seriously, words do not effectively convey this concept, because I feel like I am now living in a dream, only waiting for death so I can wake up and truly begin to live again.

The only thing I found disorienting through this whole experience was my internal clock. I could say I was out for a few seconds or a thousand years; both would seem to be correct, but neither would be accurate, as there is no way for me to understand that span of time. It seemed to take place indefinitely and simultaneously.

Since I was back in a physical body, I was again subject to time, space, internal drives, personal desires, fear, anxiety, sadness, and loneliness, but I recognized that my outlook had significantly changed, and it seemed to stay that way. I didn't see these things as permanent limitations; I now saw them as momentary distortions of consciousness. They were mere distractions and feeble attempts to disrupt my relationship with and trust in God. I still felt the love and peace of heaven, and I even endured surgery to install a pacemaker in my chest without giving into the sleep that my recent physical ordeal attempted to bring on. I refused to sleep, because I didn't want to stop thinking about the experience of heaven or stop feeling the love and peace of heaven. In fact, I was so elated that I could only think of my visit to heaven for the rest of the day (and the entire week in the hospital, for that matter). I accepted no pain medications, because I found myself so overwhelmed with God's love that I didn't need any, and I did not want my mind to be clouded by them. I was in pain, and even though my chest felt crushed from the broken ribs I sustained from the chest compressions, they did not feel as bad as I expected.

CHAPTER 18

Within an hour after coming back from death, an electrophysiologist from the hospital came to see me; he was more seasoned, experienced, and very compassionate. He explained that due to the complexity and various locations of these VTs, he felt my problems were getting worse; the sarcoids had spread throughout my entire heart, causing severe scar tissue. He said my condition was so dangerous that he needed to implant a pacemaker/defibrillator immediately. He explained that if I was to go into extended VTs, the pacemaker would pace me down by shocking my heart at a rate slightly above the VTs and physically bring it back down to a safe rhythm. He quickly deactivated my defunct defibrillator, which he said needed to be done now that he was implanting a new device and since the old one was not working effectively. He also wanted to set the lowest beats per minute to under 60 so my device would then pace me back up; this was to eliminate large gaps between my high and low BPM, which can trigger more VTs from my sarcoid-infested and scar tissue-damaged heart.

This new doctor was so kind and knowledgeable; he seemed to genuinely care about preserving my life. The decision to have a new pacemaker made the most sense after talking with him. We agreed to implant the Implantable cardioverter-defibrillator (ICD) immediately; he told me he was going directly to prepare the surgery room and assemble his team for the emergency surgery. Less than three hours after I had died, I was being transported to the operating room. This was not without risks, given all that my body had been through, but it was vitally important to get the device implanted as soon as possible, and the doctor felt I was strong enough to tolerate the surgery. More importantly, the alternative was too risky not to do it. The surgery went really well, and I was able to talk with the doctor during the procedure. I was not given sedatives because the doctor was concerned that slowing my heart rate so soon after the cardiac arrest would be dangerous. He did however answer all my questions about which step he was working on during the surgery and even talked with me about my life, sports, and other topics. I did not want to fall asleep during the surgery because I didn't want to stop thinking about the experience I had while in heaven. I resolved to remain awake despite not sleeping for the past three days and having just survived a physically exhausting experience, but I still had so much euphoria I don't think it would've been possible for me to sleep.

I was tempted by fear during the surgery. I remember thinking about how I may not make it through this, and yet I wasn't afraid of dying. I was afraid that I wouldn't have the chance to do what I came back to do. Fear is a powerful weapon, and our enemy uses it to keep us off track. Fear was trying to distract me from my experience of heaven, but it had no real power over me as long as I remained positive and trusted in God. Doing so, I found my trust in the love and peace of Jesus only grew stronger.

I realized I had just died a few hours ago and that I may still die, but I felt like I had a new lease on life and that God was the lienholder. That provided me a spark of courage that led to a full four-alarm fire in my soul. Somehow, I knew he wouldn't let me come back only to endure more pain and then die again, and yet even if he had, it would be for some greater purpose. I knew this to be true now. I now considered my life to belong fully to God and professed a desire to let him govern it as he saw fit. I was willing to do God's will and to give him complete control over whether I lived or died. What else could possibly worry me, now that I knew how much he loves us? I truly felt free of the false idea that I had control of my life anyway; for the first time in my life, I realized I never did have control over anything more than my actions. I now realized I really didn't want to control life anyway, because my life is safer in God's hands.

After surgery, I was brought back to the ICU and rested well for the rest of the day, but I did not sleep. I couldn't sleep that night, but for once, it was not from fear of shocks but because of the euphoria I felt from my

NDE. I couldn't stop contemplating how heaven had made me feel. I prayed most of the time and felt a closeness to God that I had never had in my life prior to the NDE. I still felt more connected to God than ever before, as if I was still with him.

I did finally fall asleep later that night, and even though I woke very early the next morning, I felt totally refreshed, and the excitement and the euphoria remained with me. Truthfully, I still feel the excitement and euphoria now, but living everyday life presents distractions from the excitement of my experience, and I have to reconnect with God regularly, just like everyone else.

I spent the next couple of days in the ICU on IVs, receiving powerful heart medications to prevent the VTs from continuing to threaten my life. The doctors were still concerned that I would not make it and would die again, but I responded well to the medications, and my heart and body recovered quickly. The doctors were puzzled by my quick recovery. I was no longer anxious or afraid, and I believe this was a direct result of heaven; the explanation for my quick recovery was my experiencing the love and peace of God. I knew he had plans for me and would sustain me.

CHAPTER 19

My cardiologist and electrophysiologist did not even come to visit me during this weekday; it seemed like a long stay in the hospital without much medical input. To give you more perspective, they didn't come up the three floors or even call to discuss further plans with me. Instead, they sent colleagues to check my charts and to relay apologies that they couldn't make it upstairs due to their schedules. My new doctor, however, did come by to check on me. I believe my doctors were overwhelmed with the seriousness of my condition; due to their inexperience, they were uncertain of how to proceed with such a complex diagnosis (there are few cardiac sarcoidosis experts in the world). I am sure they were embarrassed that their lack of understanding of sarcoidosis had contributed to my death. I didn't hold their ignorance of sarcoids against them, because let's face it, cardiac sarcoidosis is uncommon; few patients live through the initial event and are only diagnosed at autopsy, if at all. However, I felt they didn't even show an interest in me as a patient or a person, despite the fact that I had just died from cardiac arrest under their care.

Shortly after I was taken off the IVs and placed back on the oral medications, I has several sustained VTs, but my pacemaker successfully paced me back down to a healthy sinus rhythm. After several of these pacings and some pacing up from bradycardia (low heart beats per minute), my heart seemed to stabilize, and the gap between my highs and lows narrowed. I went into a few unsustained VTs throughout the rest of the day and into the next day, but my heart readjusted well with the medication now in my system and without much need for the pacemaker to initiate further therapy. I was then cleared to leave the ICU and step down to the cardiac unit late Wednesday afternoon. I am so thankful that my new doctor responded to my care during this event.

I continued to improve at an incredible rate over the next few days, which amazed the doctors who were working with me; they began discussing discharge. I was told I could be discharged after I had one full day without VTs. I had no control over VTs, but I certainly could control whether I stayed positive or allowed negativity to come into my being. I chose to keep the negativity out. Thursday was the first day I had no VTs, and the doctors signed off for discharge on Friday afternoon, as long as I continued to remain stable. Tina and Elijah came to pick me up from the hospital; it was clear on their faces that they had been so worried that I died and from the looks on their faces, they probably thought I might die again. Elijah hugged me with the lightest hug he has ever given me, which was unusual from him, but it felt so good anyway.

Elijah told me he was still afraid I was going to die, and tears began to fill his eyes when he and Tina began to pack me up. He seemed so shy and reserved, almost distant. Much different than his normal open and positive self. These last few months had caused an obvious change. I couldn't stand to see him this sad and concerned, so I told him that I didn't feel that I was going to die now or even in the near future. I was certain God had something else in mind for me. I told him I survived for a reason and that otherwise, I wouldn't have been allowed to make it this time. I said I had a more positive outlook on my condition and thought God wanted me to share this experience with as many other people as possible and to practice loving them. I told him how I felt great despite having died five days ago. In fact, this was the best I had felt in the last five months, and I tried to convince him to not worry, that I would only get stronger. I'm not sure how well I was able to convince him, but I was determined to show him I would live for quite a long while.

I tried to comfort Elijah by telling him about my experience; I thought the part about how I had given up the fight prior to death would show him how God has more in store for me. I said I was in terrible pain and had grown so weak that I could no longer fight, but now, I wanted to continue the fight with my new strength I received from God. I wanted to live longer since Jesus gave me the chance to come back. It almost broke my heart when he told me that if it happened again, I should just stay. He said he would be sad, but he didn't want me to suffer anymore. Perhaps he has a better understanding of life than I do.

CHAPTER 20

I returned home to many kisses and hugs, but there was a definite concern for my safety; everyone treated me like I was fragile and going to break at any moment. I could also feel some distancing of my family; they looked at me as if I was going to die any moment, and they didn't know what to do or how to act. I was still sore because of the broken ribs from the long battle to revive me, and then to top it all off, having a new device implanted in my chest. It really was a lot to physically endure, but I tried to appear as healthy as I could, for my kids' sake.

I still felt emotionally great and thought I could feel some physical improvement every day. My blood even started to feel alive again; I knew Jesus was with me, and I could feel his closeness. I really began to see how my mom's hope for a miracle was not so far-fetched; in fact, I had begun to totally buy in, because the gift of going to heaven was beyond any miracle I could've asked for. My mom stuck by me throughout this whole ordeal. I was content with whatever God had in mind for my life, and I was not setting limits on how a miracle might look. I accepted that the miracle may not be a long life or complete healing; my life belonged to him for however long it might be and for whatever purpose he might intend.

I had a hospital discharge follow-up and device check on Monday, January 23, but I did not see my doctors. My device delivered some therapy to raise my heart rate when it had fallen below 60 BPM, and that seemed to be helping to keep my heart rate more stable. Future follow-up appointments were scheduled, but not for some time. I insisted on sooner appointments to discuss my course of treatment, since my last plan was created before my Cleveland visit. I was going to get some answers from my doctors, whether they wanted to or not. The doctor who implanted the ICD had recommended that I follow up with Mayo Clinic because they were the best equipped and most accomplished hospital to treat my condition, and I wanted my doctors to set up the referrals.

I still had not had any contact with my electrophysiologist or cardiologist and my next appointment with the electrophysiologist would be February 13 (the cardiologist was not until April). Other than a brief visit when I was in the hospital in December, I had not seen them since prior to the Cleveland trip. In fact, my electrophysiologist did not answer messages I had sent inquiring about having another Holter monitor test and the referral I wanted to Mayo Clinic. I asked for this test to be performed because I knew we needed some data to know if the medications and the pacemaker were working to keep my heart stable. The more the doctors removed themselves from my care, the more I needed to rely on God to improve my heart health. I could feel my growing peace with depending on God. I was told by several doctors that it was amazing I had survived all these cardiac sarcoidosis events. I was feeling a miracle had taken place myself and that it was continuing to develop. I started to believe that perhaps keeping my doctors out of the way might be part of God's plan too.

My critical care pulmonologist reached out to Mayo Clinic and scheduled tests to provide them with a clearer picture of my conditions. I should've noted that he called me after my cardiac arrest and had been checking in with me on a weekly basis. I was scheduled for a three-day evaluation at Mayo Clinic, with a cardiac sarcoid specialist in late March. They would have scheduled me earlier, except that my ICD was not yet FDA approved for MRIs. The MRI results are important to assess the progress of my heart function due to the sarcoids and scar tissue. They also ordered a PET scan prior to the March visit and another scheduled at Mayo to make a comparison in order to evaluate the efficacy of treatment.

My critical care doctor had sent me a touching and reassuring message while I was in the hospital. He said that he was thinking about me and was sorry this had happened to me, but was ecstatic that I survived, and I could contact him anytime I needed to talk with him. He even went so far as contacting Mayo Clinic to determine what test results and medical records they needed and sent them to the Mayo team personally. He asked them what other tests could be provided here in preparation for the appointments to assist them, and he would ensure they would be completed. He scheduled the PET scan and arranged for me to get a new MRI at Mayo earlier than had been previously arranged. My critical care doctor is truly a wonderful doctor and a compassionate person. I later discovered that all my doctors at Mayo Clinic had similar philosophies to accompany their medical expertise and superior knowledge.

CHAPTER 21

On February 9, the programmer equipment for the interrogation process, which makes it possible to retrieve therapy instances from my original device, was officially recalled because it picked up radio frequencies and triggered the device to deliver an inappropriate shock. This was concerning because of the trauma it causes on a heart plagued with sarcoidosis to be shocked. My doctors didn't inform me of this recall. I found out when I went to Mayo Clinic for my MRI. I'm not sure what strike my original cardiac team would have been on at this point if this was a baseball game, but 1) sending me to Cleveland and not to Mayo Clinic was the first one, followed by 2) not scheduling a follow-up after Cleveland, 3) when they didn't spend much time on my care in December during my heart failure, 4) initially resisted my desire to diagnose the cardiac sarcoidosis, 5) not even coming up a few floors to see me after I died from cardiac arrest, 6) not scheduling a follow-up appointment after I died for one full month, and then to top it off, 7) they failed to tell me that the defibrillator they installed was now definitively known to be defective. I realized that I could no longer allow them to be involved in my care at all. That's a lot of strikes; I think they were out at this point. I only wish I would have called them out earlier in the game.

The recall explains why the device the doctor used to set my defibrillator settings or to record shocks, arrhythmias, and other cardiac events malfunctioned on October 6; after receiving false signals, I received two inappropriate shocks. Those two shocks then sent me into ventricular tachycardia, and I received a third shock. These three shocks caused an electrical storm, and I had to remain in the emergency room for several hours to stabilize. It took several more days for me to feel well enough to reattempt my recovery. On December 14, I received another shock, and again five days later, I received six more. These shocks caused a severe and noticeable decline in my health, leading eventually to my death, but it failed to deliver therapy prior to my cardiac arrest.

CHAPTER 22

I felt some pacing from my device from time to time; my settings were adjusted as my health improved, but I still didn't feel that my electrophysiologist was involved enough in my care, as he communicated mostly through nurses. I couldn't wait to get to Mayo Clinic to receive a new device. During my February appointment, my electrophysiologist suggested removing the defibrillator he had implanted back in August, because the ICD was a defibrillator as well as a pacemaker, and since the first one was now turned off due to its detrimental effects. I said that I was told that the device was recalled, and he confirmed that it was, giving me an official letter notifying patients of the recall. He said he really wanted to remove the device now that it was recalled, so a surgery date was set for March 15. This was one week prior to my big Mayo Clinic visit.

I talked to my pulmonologist, and he confirmed that my lungs and lymph nodes appeared almost completely absent of sarcoids now. This was great news because it appeared that my heart would be likely to respond the prednisone. He said that Mayo Clinic would repeat the PET scan during my visit in late March, and we may see further improvement to my heart as well, but for now, he explained that my heart was fully infested with sarcoids and what appeared to be a significant amount of scar tissue.

CHAPTER 23

A week prior to surgery, I texted my doctor and said I wanted to take my device home with me afterwards. He said I should be able to, because it was mine and I paid for it, but he thought the device manufacturer might want to look at it first. I told him that was unacceptable; I wanted it immediately after surgery, or I would just wait and have Mayo Clinic remove it. I felt that because the device manufacturer had not communicated any of the data or research they obtained from my case with me previously and didn't tell me about the recall, they should not be able to inspect my device any further without me being present and fully informed of the results. My doctor said I would have my device immediately after surgery.

I arrived early and did not see my electrophysiologist prior to my surgery. The anesthesiologist put me to sleep, and when I woke up, that ticking time bomb was no longer in my chest. I felt relieved to have it out. I have always responded well to anesthesia, and I recovered very quickly. The first thing I asked was where my device was. I did not receive it for a couple of hours after my surgery, and I wondered what tests they performed prior to returning it to me. My doctor once again did not see me after my surgery. So I received no explanation of how the procedure went or aftercare instructions. He also unexpectedly lowered my medication without explaining why. I wondered if perhaps it was having undesired side effects, even though I didn't report any and felt it was helping. I sent my doctor a text, but I did not hear from him again.

CHAPTER 24

My three days of appointments at Mayo Clinic were to begin March 20, just five days after the surgery to remove the defibrillator; my days there were full of tests. All of these tests were to determine the full extent of my condition, and they were stacked back to back, filling each of the three days. I was sore and tired, and I still felt a little like a pincushion. My appointment schedule was jam-packed with comprehensive tests. I mentioned how my previous doctor had his nurses tell me I was not having any VT events, but Mayo's Holter monitor, EKG, and device check all showed that I was indeed having regular runs of VTs and an extreme amount of PVCs. This data directly contradicted the information my doctor was communicating to me. I immediately fired him.

I was assigned a sarcoidosis cardiology team, and my new electrophysiologist recommended that I have immediate ablation surgery to stop or at least limit the VTs because a significant part of my heart was scarred and would not improve with the treatment of sarcoids. He wanted to schedule the heart ablation surgery for the first available appointment time, because he felt it was too risky to wait. He was able to schedule a surgery date of April 10 and said I could have significant relief of the VTs and PVCs, which would help me to start functioning better and see more improvement. I now had an ejection fraction of 32 percent; he felt this could be significantly improved and would improve my overall heart function. I was so happy to have a doctor willing to take on the challenge of my condition, because the scar tissue was not going to improve without immediate surgical intervention. He also discussed this treatment plan with my other doctors and was able to get them all on board and willing to participate. All but one of my doctors returned communications with the Mayo Clinic team.

My sarcoid cardiologist went over my test results in detail; he spent two hours explaining the test results and the plan moving forward. My team did not sugarcoat my condition; they told me how dire the situation was, but they assured me that they would treat my condition aggressively. They remained positive, which helped me to focus on the positive also. They told me they were surprised I made it through all that I had, considering my condition, and they felt I would be strong enough to continue to fight. They were confident that with my overall health, I had the best chance of seeing progress if the sarcoids could be controlled, and we may even see drastic improvement if we acted immediately. The part of my heart that controls the flow of oxygenated blood from the nonoxygenated blood was completely scarred and needed ablation immediately; my circulation and cardiac output was severely limited.

There were various other areas of concern, but the totality of problems would not be known until they were able to get into my heart during the surgery. This is exactly what Cleveland failed (or rather refused) to do. My cardiologist wanted to make some changes to my medications, but after consulting with my new electrophysiologist, they decided that it would be best to wait until after surgery, because they wanted me to be off the medications prior to surgery so that they could get the best electrical readings and more accurately map my scar tissue. It was nice to have a team working together and explaining the various steps in the treatment plan. I must admit, though, that I was disappointed I had such significant scar damage, because after my visit to heaven, I had secretly hoped that God was going to heal it. Perhaps it's even more of a miracle that I was functioning as well as I was, despite the significant scar tissue. I began to wonder if God wasn't directly sustaining my heart function. I was relieved that my Mayo doctors were so quick to act and were treating my condition so decisively, not simply ignoring it and leaving me to die. I was excited about the possibilities of recovery.

I was tired from three packed days of appointments and sore from being pricked and prodded like a voodoo doll of someone who was really disliked. I was optimistic, though, because I felt they were being thorough with these tests. My heart proved to be healthy mechanically, except for the sarcoids and scar damage it had caused. I had no mechanical damage and no underlying cardiovascular disease, so successful recovery was likely to increase with the ablation surgery.

The next two weeks waiting for the surgery made me nervous because my last attempt to receive ablation was the horrible experience in Cleveland. I had endured so much from the hospitalization after the six shocks I received just one week after the Cleveland appointments. I then had a cardiac arrest; I was scared but looked forward to the heart ablation surgery and knew that it was part of God's plan for me, I knew he would ensure that I made it to the surgery and that the surgery would be successful. All I had to do was to wait to get there, follow through with the procedure, and work hard toward recovery.

CHAPTER 25

The night before the surgery, I stayed in a hotel across from the hospital entrance, so I could walk over the following morning (I had to report at 5:30 a.m.). I didn't sleep well the night before surgery, knowing that I would be in for a long surgery and a painful recovery. After I arrived and checked in, I was escorted up to the surgery prep rooms; they gave me a gown and began pre-op procedures. I was brought into the pre-op room and met with the anesthesiologist, who informed me that she would be giving me something to sleep but couldn't give me any pain medications because it might dull my heart reactions to the stimulus to produce VTs. This would cause me to feel extreme pain when I woke up; she just wanted me to know to expect it and be aware that it was a normal reaction and not my heart being in worse shape.

I was scared, but every step of the procedure was thoroughly explained to me, along with the rationale for that step and how we would adjust if needed. I was wheeled into the operating room and introduced to everyone present; they were so friendly, and I immediately felt at ease. I was praying to God for protection and a successful surgery as the anesthesia was administered, and I soon became drowsy and drifted off to sleep. I would spend over eight hours in that operating room, as the surgery was very extensive. When I woke up, I was in the ICU; I was told that some additional steps in the plan had to be performed because of the complexity of my condition. I was assured that the surgery went well, and I was going to be okay, but I was in a lot of pain.

My doctor came in and told me he had to perform several ablations to both ventricles and to the outside of my heart, as the damage was very extensive. I had to have cardioversion performed several times. Then he decided he had ablated enough and didn't want to risk further trauma to my heart, as it had been through so much at that point. He explained that I would need to stay in the ICU that night to have all my wounds cared for properly. I had two entry wounds, one on each side of my groins; I had a catheter in my chest, which had to be drained as it filled with fluid; and I had a catheter in my wrist. I now really looked like a voodoo doll and felt like one too.

My care team was awesome. My other cardiac sarcoidosis specialist came by at the end of her day, on her way home, just to check in on me. It was nice to have a care team that really cared. I had the best nursing care in the ICU. The first nurse provided me so much comfort as I came out of the fog of surgery and helped me to reorientate, then when his shift ended, his replacement took over where he left off. I was not allowed to take any sleep medication because my blood pressure was so low after surgery, so I spent the entire night awake; my nurse checked on me regularly and talked with me as much as he could to make me more comfortable. He got me juice, Jell-o, and ice cream to make my night a little more comfortable.

I had to have my chest drained every couple of hours, which was a painful process and made for a long night. I was told I would not be cleared to leave the ICU until I was under a certain fluid volume for two consecutive withdrawals. When the fluid was extracted, I could feel the pain around my heart and in the back of my neck toward my left shoulder. The pain was intensified because of my having endured so many cardioversions during surgery and the devices implanted in my chest. I was moved to the cardiac unit the next evening. I was disappointed because I would not be getting out of the hospital as soon as I had hoped.

Since August 27, 2016, through all of 2017, I have had a cardiac arrest and four heart failures, been to the emergency room six times, had five ambulance rides, and been in the hospital thirteen times for a total of thirty-four days. I have had thirteen surgeries and received twenty-three shocks to restore my heart. I underwent treatment every three months at Mayo, but by the end of 2017, my condition has not responded to treatment and had continue to worsen. Part of me had expected to have a miraculous recovery after having been in heaven, but God truly does work in mysterious ways, as the saying goes. I learned that even though my condition looked grim from a medical standpoint, and it worsened from when it had already killed me once, I was still improving mentally and spiritually. I felt that God had sustained me despite my physical limitations. For the first time in my life, I was depending on someone other than myself, and God was making me feel whole because of it.

I was not afraid of death and no longer felt that I was going to immediately die. Of course, I had no proof of this. I never asked God how much extra time I would be given. It was just a feeling, and it was accompanied by a strong belief that I had more to do on earth. But the best feeling was that I was no longer afraid to die. Death held no power over me.

Since that first ablation, I had several more heart failures, and in January 2018, my doctors requested a new and experimental medication therapy that would require me to have at least two infusions, twice a month, every six months. My insurance initially denied this treatment, as they claimed it was not medically necessary, but they approved it after further explanation from my doctors. I had the infusions, and it seemed to have caused my other organs to go into remission, but my heart was still unresponsive. My condition worsened, and treatment up to August 2018 seemed ineffective due to the severity of my disease and scar damage. In September 2018, I was evaluated and recommended for a heart transplant. The lessons I learned in heaven had helped me to endure the pain and uncertainty of this world, and I believed I would receive the right heart at the right time if it was what was best for me; otherwise, something else would occur. My life had become more important than just getting through it; I had learned to live it, no matter how limited I was.

CHAPTER 26

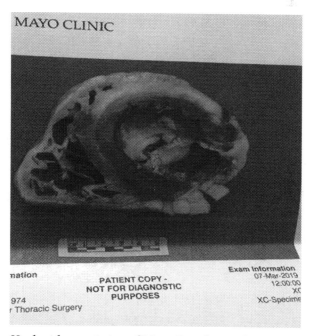

God kept me alive until March 6, 2019, when a suitable heart became available for transplant. When doctors at the Mayo Clinic Transplant Program reviewed my heart's biopsy after the transplant, they told me it was a medical miracle that my heart could still function. It was even more astounding that I was alive, let alone having lived as long as I did with my heart in the condition it was in. I have attached a picture of my heart at biopsy so that you can grasp the seriousness of the damage to my heart and to show how only by my heart resting in God's loving hand, did I survive until transplant.

From August 27, 2016, to May 2019, I was hospitalized approximately fifty times, and I had hundreds of tests, treatments, and evaluations. I have had a truly blessed recovery since my transplant. I had no rejection at all, and all my other organs are working well. God has given me the additional time to live life, which he allowed me to choose. I am so grateful for the generous donor and his family, and I pray every day for blessings for the kindness and love they showed to me as another of God's creations. This experience, as painful and full of suffering as it has been, was the most wonderful experience of my entire life. Even though the two years that I suffered after the cardiac arrest were the most physically, emotionally, and mentally painful and exhausting times of my life, I was able to stay positive and feel God's love and peace. I never gave up hope or stopped being happy because of the gift of the NDE and spending time with God in heaven.

The experience of being given a new heart showed me that how I spent my life previously was not conducive to happiness and not even close to the pure joy of heaven. I was always trying to improve my career, make more money, and increase my stature in the eyes of others, but what I ultimately learned was that those were simply distractions keeping me from finding what was truly important. I learned that I really missed God, and I also missed his people. I learned to live my life with my fullest focus on God and his will for me and showing his love to others, no matter the cost or how severe the consequences may be; this is the only way to sustain happiness and find meaning in this life. I will strive to serve the Lord with all my heart and to love his people for the rest of the days he has given me.

I have been an organ donor for my entire adult life, but I never thought much about it. I had always thought, *Why wouldn't I donate life to someone else when mine had come to an end?* It's not like I can take it with me. It was freely given to me, so I felt like I should freely give it to another who is in need. But receiving the gift of life from someone is truly a blessing, and I will be forever grateful.

CHAPTER 27

Conclusion and Great Wisdom on Living Life and Dying with Grace

So live your life that the fear of death can never enter your
heart. Trouble no one about their religion; respect others in
their view, and demand that they respect yours. Love your life,
perfect your life, beautify all things in your life. Seek to make
your life long and its purpose in the service of your people.
Prepare a noble death song for the day when you go over the great
divide. Always give a word or a sign of salute when meeting or passing
a friend, even a stranger, when in a lonely place. Show respect to all
people and bow to none. When you arise in the morning, give thanks
for the food and for the joy of living. If you see no reason for giving
thanks, the fault lies only in yourself. Abuse no one and nothing, for
abuse turns the wise ones to fools and robs the spirit of its vision.
When it comes your time to die, be not like those whose hearts are
filled with fear of death, so that when their time comes they weep
and pray for a little more time to live their lives over again in a
different way. Sing your death song and die like a hero going home.
—Tecumseh

Lessons Learned in Heaven

Highly challenging moments in our lives, the ones that truly cause us pain and force action, are often accompanied by suffering, and yet they somehow seem to turn out to be the moments that shape and define our character and make us better people. Afterwards, it becomes obvious that who we are soon becomes an accumulation of these highly impactful moments; without them, we would not be the same person. As we often pray for them to stop or to never occur to begin with, I wonder if we would really like who we would have been without them. If we dislike what we have become and wish to change, then we need to make choices that define and support the type of person we wish to be after these moments. Those challenging moments require difficult actions and provide us with incredible skills, experience, and beautiful characteristics, if we act honorably.

Deep in our human hearts is a hole wishing to be filled, but nothing in this world can fill it. It was like the vast, empty space I saw when I first arrived in heaven, but when I returned, I did not see the dark hole. Instead, I saw my life at the end of the portal. God had filled that hole with his love. I felt my heart filled in heaven, but even now, in the absence of God's presence, my hole has not returned. This is because everything in this world is temporary, and once we have acquired it, the time of its enjoyment begins to count down, until we become accustomed to possessing it. We soon need to acquire something new to temporarily fill the hole once again. Only God can permanently fill the hole because it is caused by the lack of his eternal essence, which is how we gained our existence. That hole is like an empty void within us, and I think it is the black darkness I first saw in heaven, but if we turn toward God and go to him, he will always fill it. He will fill it so full that it begins to overflow, and our joy will be truly great, no matter what circumstance we find ourselves in.

I have since learned that the path to God goes through the dark tunnel; it is literally the path of love. Love is the only thing that can support us through the darkness. If death is like sleep or some kind of nothingness, then we will not know anyway, as our consciousness would cease to exist, but as I learned, through God's great love, death leads to a life truly greater than we currently know. Only then will we be truly awake. Once we are awake, we should help others wake up too. When we go trudging through life, we must remember those who are suffering and be at their sides to help them make the way through the darkness. When God said, "Let there be light," he was introducing consciousness and life into the world. And when I saw the light shining into the darkness of that immense void, my consciousness grew exponentially. That dark void I used to have is now full of light.

Material things that we own can become great distractions and often end up owning us. In the Army, we would often go on a ruck march; you learn quickly that what you put into your pack becomes a reminder of the things you don't really need, as the weight of that pack bears down upon you, trying to prevent you from reaching your destination and accomplishing your goal. During that march, you would give anything to get rid of some of that stuff. The things we own or desire in life have the same effect, as they try to prevent us from reaching our true destination, weighing us down to this world and blocking our connection with God. They try to prevent us from making our way down the path of love, through that dark tunnel and into God's wondrous light.

The world and all its traps can sneak up on us, and over time, it often overtakes us. It's like when you put a frog into a pan of hot water, it will jump out, but if you want to cook it, then you just have to put it in warm water and turn up the heat slowly, raising the temperature and cooking the frog without it even realizing it, until it's too late. That is how the temptations that the world provides ensnares us. I no longer want to live that way, satisfied with the slow death of complacency. Returning to life after seeing heaven wasn't a simple choice, either. I still have to work at keeping the distractions the world offers at bay, but knowing God's love and being awake now make it harder for the world to cook me. Deep in our hearts is that hole wanting to be filled, but nothing in this world can fill it. We are unable to truly experience love without God, and only he can fill that void.

My shame at relying on my own skills and abilities made my relationship with God hard to reestablish, so I buried myself in my ambition. This became a vicious circle and made it hard for me to believe he would forgive me; I couldn't fully appreciate his love for me. In my work, I believe in the redemptive qualities of human beings, but I couldn't see why God should feel this way toward me, after all I had done.

I always found a sense of significance from protecting others, but in heaven, I didn't feel powerful, and no one needed my protection. However, I felt more significant than I ever felt before. Instead of feeling like a protector, I felt protected and loved beyond any measure I can describe. I felt that God loved me, that he truly loved me, and he only loved me for being me. I didn't have to earn it; I don't know why he gave me this wonderful experience. The only thing he wanted in return was love from me. I found that my walk down that dark tunnel made it impossible not to give him love, as I could feel the overwhelming love from him. It was totally rewarding to have this connection of love with God. I don't know who gets into heaven, but it didn't feel like he wanted to turn anyone away. Seriously, God let me in, and I am nowhere near perfect.

Death is hard to explain, difficult to describe, and even harder to understand, because few people have experienced it and then told about it. We think in terms of our life experiences and form our understanding of existence from these experiences and what we can see. I was knocked out twice during my life, but neither time did I have any thoughts or dreams; everything just went black. The same lack of consciousness took place every time I had surgery and even when I had my heart failure events, but when I died, I never lost conscious thought for a second. I knew what was happening and what I was experiencing the whole time. When we die, life does not stop, just like when we get knocked out. The obvious difference is that when we die, we actually start to live more vibrantly than ever before, and we are fully aware of it. Dying was the greatest experience of my life.

I have always believed in human souls, heaven, God, and Jesus, but I thought all examples of NDEs could be justified by scientific explanations, such as the death surge (the death surge is when your brain theoretically releases all of your neurotransmitters prior to death, creating a surge in brain wave activities). This is what I thought happened to people who said they had an NDE. I think proponents of this theory are forgetting about the body's first line of defense again pain and suffering, which is commonly known as shock. The brain surge and shock are incompatible, because they cause two different reactions. I will not fault you if you doubt my story, but I hope you believe in the amazing experience I was privileged to have.

Remember my doctors were perplexed by my condition and out of options; Tina and I were told to focus on quality of life, not quantity, and in the end, I had given up and died. Jesus renewed my spirit, improved my quality of life, and gave me some more quantity to go with it all. The fact that I am writing this story now is a testament to God's power and grace. It is the miracle my mom talked of (even if it's not how she thought it would look). Most people with cardiac sarcoidosis don't live to talk about it, especially when it is as bad as mine. The extra time I've been given is such a precious gift, and the fact that my consciousness never stopped during my NDE is a wonderful experience that I wouldn't trade for anything. I am glad I died and was privileged in such a way.

Showing more love to others seems to be the only purpose worth having now. It has become my personal mission that I hope to focus on for the rest of my life. I think of the love I received from others throughout my life but failed to fully recognize. Experiencing God's love the way I did opened my heart to not only give love but to also receive it. That is how love works; it is meant to flow freely. I am grateful for the support of my family, friends, and even wonderful strangers throughout my lengthy battle, which I continue to face every day.

The feelings that I carried back from the other side provide me so much peace and understanding that I feel like I could endure anything. I am able to endure the extreme pain I found myself in for so long. I now actually look at the time I was dead as a kindness and a relief from this world, but I am determined to make the most of my second chance and the extra time I've been provided. I will not be like the person who is arriving late to an interview and prays, "God, please if you let me find a parking spot, I will never drink, smoke, or swear ever again." They pull into the lot and immediately find a spot near the front door and say, "Never mind, I'll take care of this one myself."

I experienced something so wonderful and so life-changing that I will not waste it. And when I die again, as I certainly will, I will go bravely and with a euphoric heart to be with God.

The Prayer of St. Francis

Lord, make me an instrument of your peace,
where there is hatred, let me sow love;
where there is injury, pardon;
where there is doubt, faith;
where there is despair, hope;
where there is darkness, light;
where there is sadness, joy.

O Divine Master,
Grant that I may not so much seek
to be consoled as to console;
to be understood as to understand;
to be loved as to love.
For it is in giving that we receive;
it is in pardoning that we are pardoned;
and it is in dying that we are born to eternal life.

Printed in the United States
By Bookmasters